# The Suddenly Successful Student & Friends

## A Guide to Overcoming Learning & Behavior Problems

### How Behavioral Optometry Helps

#### 4th Edition

Hazel R. Dawkins
Ellis Edelman, O.D.
Constantine Forkiotis, O.D.

The Optometric Extension Program
Foundation

The OEP Foundation, founded in 1928, is an international non-profit organization dedicated to continuing education and research for the advancement of human progress through education in behavioral vision care.
OEP Foundation, Inc.
1921 E. Carnegie Ave., Suite 3-L
Santa Ana, CA 92705
www.oep.org
Managing editor: Sally Marshall Corngold
Cover design: Kathleen Patterson

Library of Congress Cataloging-in-Publication Data
Dawkins, Hazel H. Richmond.
  The suddenly successful student & friends : behavioral optometry in the 21st century helping overcome learning, health & behavior problems / Hazel R. Dawkins, Ellis Edelman, Constantine Forkiotis. -- 4th ed.
    p. cm.
  Includes bibliographical references and index.
  ISBN 978-0-929780-25-2 (alk. paper)
  1. Behavioral optometry--Popular works.  I. Edelman, Ellis S., 1924- II. Forkiotis, Constantine, 1923- III. Title. IV. Title: Suddenly successful student and friends.
  RE960.D38 2009
  617.7'5--dc22
                                    2009036148
************************************************
Optometry is the health care profession specifically licensed by state law to prescribe lenses, optical devices and procedures to improve human vision. Optometry has advanced vision therapy as a unique treatment modality for the development and remediation of the visual process. Effective vision therapy requires extensive understanding of:
  • the effects of lenses (including prisms, filters and occluders)
  • the variety of responses to the changes produced by lenses
  • the various physiological aspects of the visual process
  • the pervasive nature of the visual process in human behavior
As a consequence, effective vision therapy requires the supervision, direction and active involvement of the optometrist.
************************************************

# Contents

# Preface

The changes in behavioral optometry in the quarter of a century since the publication of this book's predecessor have been considerable. This in itself is not unusual—what hasn't changed since the 1980s? Yet the bottom line for this optometric specialty is the same that it always has been: dedicated professionals persevering in the face of little recognition and scant reward, other than that enormous intangible, the satisfaction of helping others. The problems that can be mitigated may be difficulty learning to read, ADD, autism, crippling migraines or traumatic brain injury. Practitioners who offer optometric vision therapy are, in short, amazing men and women. Some are visionaries, some are geniuses, all are tireless in their therapeutic work.

I can make this bold statement because I am not an optometrist. Rather, I, my family and many of my friends have been on the receiving end of this beneficial therapy and know firsthand how valuable it is. And, as a writer, I took up the challenge issued by my co-author Dr. Ellis Edelman, when first I suggested I write a small book for the consumer.

"Go visit other optometrists," he said. So I followed this excellent advice. The quest began with a train trip from Philadelphia to New York City to sit with the legendary Dr. Elliott Forrest as he examined patients at the Infants' Vision Clinic at the College of Optometry, State University of New York. Dr. Forrest gave me copies of his papers and invited me to return. I did, many times. Eventually, my travels included visits with more practitioners in New York, California, France, England and Australia. Probably I won't actually visit Japan or South Africa or much of Europe, but I have been in touch with many optometrists in the forty countries where this health therapy is available.

My second co-author, Dr. Gus Forkiotis, was as generous with his time as Dr. Edelman. Until his recent death, Gus and I were in constant touch and I learned much from this gifted practitioner. Whether asking me to work with him and Dr. E. Bertolli on articles for the mainstream media (so far, our overtures have been rejected) or having me edit papers for diverse journals, from the *Police Chief* to the *Forensic Examiner* and *Counterterrorism*, Gus supplied me with a steady stream of valuable information. I sorely miss our lunches, telephone conversations and frequest exchange of e-mails.

Over the years, I have come to appreciate more and more what Dr. Forrest explained to me in the early 1980s: Our mental states, beliefs, biases and attitudes are highly involved in creating what we are and what we become, visually and otherwise. Examine that from another perspective and you understand that your vision is the prime factor that guides your perception of life.

Hazel Dawkins
Greenfield, Massachusetts

# Introduction

We were lucky as parents. Our son was four and our daughter an infant when I joined the staff of the Southern California College of Optometry. Unlike most parents, the importance of good vision and quality vision care surrounded us during our children's early development. Both children wore bifocals in elementary school and as far as I know never experienced any social stigma because of it. Both received vision therapy from competent behavioral optometrists in our home community. The optometrists, Drs. Beth Ballinger and Steve Cohen, always had time to discuss their care with us and kept us informed of progress. We did the prescribed home activities, as much as possible in a busy family setting. Any long-term visual problems they might have experienced were prevented. Both my wife and I are highly nearsighted and according to conventional wisdom our genetics should have passed a similar condition on to our children. This did not happen and I am convinced it was because of the preventive care they received, because we knew what to look for and what to do. Like I said, we were lucky.

Many parents just don't know that vision impacts every aspect of their lives and their children's lives. ***The purpose of vision is to direct action.*** That simple statement sums up the importance of *The Suddenly Successful Student & Friends* to all parents as well as educators and other professionals working with children. We take in information through an efficient and well functioning visual system. From that information we take appropriate action to meet the demands of every situation, be it in a classroom, on a sporting field or while driving a vehicle. If the information received is not accurate or cannot be processed in an accurate, timely manner, our action or reaction to the information will be faulty. This can result in a child being a poor reader, being clumsy, missing a pass or a ground ball, or more importantly misjudging distances between vehicles in a parking lot or on the highway.

Seeking and obtaining quality vision care from an optometrist who understands visual function and visual processing is vitally important. The authors of this book, Drs. Edelman and Forkiotis and Mrs. Dawkins, provide clear signs and symptoms of possible vision problems that can be corrected. They then guide the reader in seeking and finding quality vision care from an appropriate doctor of optometry. Please note the quote from Nobel Prize winning scientist Dr. David Hubel on page 33. It bears repeating: *"If an ophthalmologist or optometrist tells you this [that it is too late for the adult vision system to change] you should find somebody else."*

I would suggest a corollary for parents of children struggling in school for no obvious reason. If your child is not performing to his or her ability, and an ophthalmologist or optometrist tells you that vision is not a problem because she has 20/20 sight, find somebody else. Subtle problems with alignment or tracking skills can lead to major learning problems as the child transitions from *learning to read* to *reading to learn.*

The visual demands on our lives, from early childhood through retirement are increasing exponentially. We are suited for distance seeing by nature. Only in the last hundred years or so have we brought our world indoors and at nearpoint. Hunter's eyes do not serve us well on a laptop or a Blackberry.

**Vision is the key to learning; learning is the key to earning.**

*The Suddenly Successful Student & Friends* can be your key to understanding the need for quality vision care and the ultimate success in school and in life.


Robert A. Williams
Santa Ana, California

# 1

# A Parents' and Teachers' Guide to Vision Problems

If you are a parent or a teacher, you know firsthand the challenges students face in the 21st century, with its myriad dramatic changes. The speed of communications increases at a dizzying rate and computers, video games and cell phones are in constant, intense use. The Internet arrived in our lives like a tsunami, offering its seductive 24/7 access and even if you are not one of the 1.5 billion Internet users worldwide (the number grows exponentially), chances are you don't need be told what it means to "Google" information.

This incredibly rapid pace of life puts new pressures on us. It can be hard to recognize some of the demands, particularly those on youngsters, whose vision systems—like much of the rest of their bodies—develop over the first ten to twelve years of their lives.

**About ten million children under the age of twelve in the United States have vision problems that make it hard for them to cope with home and school.**

*That's the bad news.* It's from sources such as the National Institute of Child Health and Human Development and the American Optometric Association (AOA), the nation's leading professional organization devoted to the problems of vision and vision care. The warning is clear. AOA reminds us that it is well documented that youngsters with vision problems usually have difficulties with learning in school. They often have trouble dealing with family and friends. They may become so frustrated by their problems that they retreat into rebellion. They can become dropouts. Suicides. Or menaces to society.

AOA has made an important distinction between *vision* and *sight*, explaining that vision conditions rarely threaten a child's sight. However, poor vision often prevents a child's development into a normal, contributing adult by interfering with learning, inhibiting participation in sports and creating frustration.

If a child's vision is not adequate to the many demands in each day, a variety of problems from headaches to unruly behavior can be triggered.

*The good new is this:* In almost every case of a child with a vision problem, there is a relatively simple solution. It can be supplied by a doctor of optometry who specializes in vision therapy. As a result, health, learning and behavior problems are helped and a child can then respond to other therapies such as remedial education or counseling, which might not have been effective before optometric vision therapy.

*The trick is:* Recognizing the child with the problem and getting the child to the correct practitioner. Parents, teachers, all of us need to know the difference between sight and vision.

**Sight is the ability to see, to look at an object and have it in focus.**

**Vision is the ability to understand what is seen. Vision is how we form our perception of the world and what is happening around us. When we use our vision, the brain organizes the information seen and gives it meaning, often by relating it to our other senses and past experience.**

**Vision develops in a sequence of predictable stages during the first 12 years of life. It is shaped by genetics, health, your experiences and the environment.**

**Vision can therefore be trained.**

Sight and vision are not the same; there is a critical difference between them. Sight is the ability of the eyes to focus, one of the many different skills that make up vision. When skills such as convergence, fixation and teaming integrate efficiently with the brain's visual cortex so that you understand what you see, the result is vision.

## True, Their Eyesight May Be Good
## But Is Their Vision in Trouble?

As a parent or a teacher, you must be able to make this distinction. Most children have healthy eyes. They can score an easy 20/20 on the eye charts. Even if one eye is a little near- or farsighted and the other is not. That is "sight."

Vision, however, is another thing. If, for instance, one eye is a little nearsighted and the other eye a little farsighted, they are not able to work together as a team. The message they send to the brain is confusing. One eye delivers one message to the brain, the other eye delivers another.

To a child, this is like being told by the father to do one thing and by the mother to do another. So the child is faced with a dilemma. Which parent—which eye message—to follow? When a child's brain is confused by contradictory messages from the eyes, the body becomes a battleground. Under the most extreme circumstances, the brain makes one of several choices. The two discussed here are radical decisions:

1. the brain stops accepting messages from one eye;

2. the brain alternates reception from one eye to the other; this slows understanding and creates confusion.

This failure of the eyes to work together as a team is called, appropriately enough, "lack of teaming." Once discovered, the child needs to visit a doctor of optometry who specializes in optometric vision care. Lack of teaming is only one of a number of vision problems that affect learning and behavior. Spotting the symptoms of such vision problems is a challenge for parents and teachers.

As technology shatters its own records and new electronic devices are marketed, we have more challenges, more stress. This translates into ever greater demands on our vision systems. Optometric vision therapy continues to offer solutions, even as the situations intensify.

## Do Adults Have Problems Triggered
## by Vision Imbalances?

What about students over the age of twelve—or adults, for that matter?  The sad truth is that at least a portion of the individuals in any school, college or office have learning, work and health difficulties (health issues range from chronic headaches to high levels of stress or hyperactivity, mood swings, depression and other challenges).  Typically, undetected vision imbalances trigger such problems.  Usually, an optometrist who offers optometric vision therapy can help remediate vision imbalances and this in turn opens the way for improvements in learning, work and health difficulties.

**Age does not determine whether you can benefit from optometric vision therapy.  Infants of two months can be helped, so can adults—whatever their age.***

---

*Among other studies, see the 2008 update & 2004 revision of Dr. Steve Hokoda's 1985 research, "General binocular dysfunctions in an urban optometry clinic." *Journal of the American Optometric Association* 1985;7:560-62.

# 2

# Why Do Children Fail?

*"Mariana can't read, gets headaches watching TV."*
*"Diane, a fourth grader, can hardly get through a simple first-grade book."*
*"Derek is 14, surly, unfriendly. On his way to being a dropout. Still can't read."*
*"Carlos has terrible migraine headaches, often cuts school. His family is really worried."*

Those are some of the concerns that bring parents to doctors of optometry. Teachers say, "Learn to read, then read to learn." But how can you read to learn if you can't learn to read? Does the problem go away after students leave school? Not in the U.S., where 30 million (14% of adults) are unable to perform simple and everyday literacy activities.

How many theories have we heard about why students struggle to read? How many strategies and programs have been aimed at helping them learn to read? A staggering amount. Yet the U.S. and other countries considered world leaders still have unacceptably high levels of illiteracy. In the U.K., the *Daily Telegraph* of 14 June, 2006, reported that one in six British adults lack the literacy skills of an 11-year-old. Every year, 100,000 pupils in the U.K. leave school functionally illiterate.

Although their article (*Journal of Behavioral Optometry 2007;*18:72) focuses on research for a study of reading-related problems in mild traumatic brain injury, Drs. K. J. Ciuffreda and N. Kapoor start by explaining that "Reading is a complex activity involving a range of functions and abilities, including oculomotor, sensory, cognitive and attention aspects, as well as their integration."

It's true that learning to read isn't easy but consider this: If you have vision problems, the task becomes almost impossible.

## In Her Own Words

**April C.** Age 23.

> *I never really thought I had any problems or difficulties that were significant.... I was a bright child but didn't like doing schoolwork. I liked reading but fell asleep all the time doing it. I got nauseous easily from car rides or too much movement. But so did lots of other people! I had trouble understanding what I read for homework but my teachers and I figured it was that I didn't like the content, or I was just lazy. My attention span was very short. Headaches were common. This was just part of growing up, right? Apparently I was wrong. I had a regular eye exam with Dr. Harris [an optometrist in Maryland] and he suggested vision therapy. I worked for several weeks and suddenly I was comprehending written material and verbal instructions much better. My headaches stopped. I am much less nauseous from car rides and movement. Life feels so much easier. I didn't even realize that my life was harder than it had to be. I feel so much better about myself now knowing that I wasn't "lazy" but had vision problems that are so common or have such slight symptoms that they are undetected or chalked up to laziness. I almost wish I could go back and do school all over again, knowing I now have the skills I lacked. Almost.*

In general, preschool children have good vision. Nevertheless, a small percentage of preschoolers have existing vision system problems. These can come from illnesses like measles or influenza. High fever, eye or head injury or pregnancy complications may also be factors. The fact is the majority of vision problems go unrecognized until the pressures of schoolwork and study begin to overload the vision system. The sudden impact of "nearpoint" work (reading, writing, drawing, doing numbers, using a computer) causes changes. A tendency to nearsightedness or farsightedness will become more pronounced. An eye may begin to cross or drift. Sight may become blurred or the child may begin to see double.

**Most vision imbalances are triggered or aggravated by stress—often by the visual demands of schoolwork or by computer use.**

This is a complication for parents and teachers because changes in children's vision usually happen so gradually that few children are aware of them. They assume that everyone sees the same way as they do. This can be wildly misleading to the adults in their lives because children may have blurred sight or be seeing double and it will never occur to them to describe the condition.

That's why parents and teachers have to be alert to all the possible vision problems.

The kind of learning, behavior and health difficulties we are talking about probably will not be uncovered in the typical school eye chart examination or by an examination that is limited to checking eye health and eyesight. A thorough vision exam by a doctor of optometry whose expertise is optometric vision care is wise. Here are some of the warning clues that can be seen readily.

## How to Spot a Vision Imbalance

**Signs You Can Observe**

- Crossed or turned eyes;
- Reddened, watering, burning or itching eyes; encrusted eyelids, frequent sties;
- Turning or tilting of the head to use one eye only, or closing or covering one eye;
- Placing head close to book or desk when reading or writing;
- Frowning or scowling while reading or writing;
- Excessive blinking or rubbing of the eyes;
- Losing the place while reading and using finger or marker to guide eyes;
- Spidery, excessively sloppy or hard-to-read handwriting or writing that becomes smaller and crowded or inconsistent in size.

**Related to Behavior**

- Short attention span for the child's age;

- Nervousness, irritability, restlessness or unusual fatigue after visual concentration;
- Displaying evidence of developmental or emotional immaturity;
- Low frustration level; withdrawn, has difficulty getting along with other children;
- Headaches, nausea and dizziness;
- Complaints of blurring of vision or of double vision at any time.

**Related to Classroom Work**
- Saying words aloud or lip reading;
- Difficulty remembering what is read;
- Omitting or repeating words or confusing similar words;
- Persistent word reversals after second grade; difficulty remembering, identifying and reproducing basic geometric forms;
- Difficulty following verbal instructions;
- Poor eye-hand coordination when copying from the chalkboard, throwing or catching a ball, buttoning clothing or tying shoes.

If you notice such symptoms—and they can be subtle—you will be doing the child a lifetime service by calling on the expertise of an optometrist who offers optometric vision therapy, the specialist equipped to diagnose and treat vision-related problems. A wealth of reputable scientific studies validates the efficiency of optometry vision care (see Ch. 8 and the Appendix). Imbalances of the vision system cannot always be corrected by the commonly prescribed eyeglasses or contact lenses. But optometric vision care, either lenses alone or in combination with the therapy, can be effective in helping youngsters acquire the necessary vision skills.

## Helpful Advice

Years ago, Allan Cott, M.D, a psychiatrist and best-selling author, said that when learning, health and behavior problems are vision-related, optometric vision therapy can help the individual make changes and improvements to the vision system. This in turn will provide the individual with a firm foundation for beneficial change in other areas. His words ring true, loud and clear, today.

# 3

# Care for Your Vision: Who Can Help?

The *Journal of Behavioral Optometry* states that, "Optometry is the health care profession specifically licensed by state law to prescribe lenses, optical devices and procedures to improve human vision. Optometry has advanced vision therapy as a unique treatment modality for the development and remediation of the visual process. Effective vision therapy requires extensive understanding of the:

- effects of lenses (including prisms, filters and occluders);
- variety of responses to the changes produced by lenses;
- various physiological aspects of the visual process;
- pervasive nature of the visual process and human behavior.

As a consequence, effective vision therapy requires the supervision, direction and active involvement of the optometrists."

Two kinds of doctors specialize in eye care. There is the Doctor of Optometry (O.D.); we know this doctor as the "optometrist." The other kind of eye doctor is the Doctor of Ophthalmology (M.D.). We know this doctor as the "ophthalmologist."

**The O.D. degree** is earned after a minimum of seven years of college and graduate education. The four-year program at colleges of optometry includes biochemistry, human anatomy, endocrinology and microbiology, general pharmacology and pathology, sensory and perceptual psychology and clinic work. The American Optometric Association reports that there are some 37,000 "full time equivalent" optometrists in the U.S. (i.e., roughly 30,000 full time practitioners and 14,000 part-timers, who equal 7,000 full time optometrists).

Within optometry, you can find general optometrists as well as practitioners who specialize in contact lenses, sports, pediatric, geriatric
or behavioral optometry. The latter is an umbrella term for optometrists who may describe their work as developmental or functional;
these specialists in optometry are qualified to offer optometric vision
therapy. In the next few paragraphs, you will find details on the
different kinds of doctors who specialize in eye care. Keep in mind
the difference between sight and vision.

**The General Optometrist** offers valuable general eye health care
and refraction (the clinical measurement of the eye to determine
the need for lenses). All optometrists are trained to give excellent
primary health care. Extensive education prepares optometrists
to detect not only ocular disease but also signs of certain health
problems such as hypertension, diabetes and arteriosclerosis.

**The Behavioral, Developmental or Functional Optometrist**
has postdoctoral training in optometric vision therapy. In
contrast to the general optometrist and the ophthalmologist, who
usually believe that visual problems stem from random or genetic
biological variations, these specialists believe that visual problems are also triggered by environmental factors which may be
developmental or induced by stress.

**The Ophthalmologist** is the other kind of eye doctor. A medical
doctor (M.D.) whose training is in diseases of the eye and eye
surgery, ophthalmologists also examine eyes and prescribe lenses
but their specialty is in surgery and treating diseases of the eyes.

**The Optician** is a licensed technician who produces and/or
dispenses the optical lenses, glasses or other equipment prescribed
by optometrists and ophthalmologists.

For many years, all states in the U.S. have licensed optometrists to
prescribe drugs for the ocular system. The American optometrists
who pioneered the development of optometric vision therapy did
so without the use of drugs. However, optometrists like Dr. Nancy
Torgerson of Seattle, Washington, and Dr. Tirsa Quinones (she
moved her practice to Puerto Rico from Connecticut) explain that
they and many of their colleagues have taken the rigorous licensing

exams because of their desire to understand the effects of drugs on the human system.

"This knowledge increases my ability to work more efficiently with ophthalmologists and other M.D.s who prescribe medication for patients referred to me," Dr. Quinones said. "All optometrists have this type of training during their college years, but the number of drugs has increased and so much more is known about their effect and interaction. Much will depend on the type of practice an optometrist has, but I felt it would enhance my ability to offer the best type of optometric vision therapy possible."

## The Wise Choice

Parents and teachers need to turn to the optometrist who specializes in behavioral, functional or developmental vision therapy when they suspect a student has a vision problem, based on the symptoms described in Chapter 2. The truth is that it's never too late for anyone, regardless of age, to seek optometric vision care, as you can read in the amazing case history of "Stereo Sue" in Chapter 6. Numerous scientific studies over the decades have validated optometric vision therapy for youngsters and adults (see Chapter 8 and the Scientific Studies in the Appendix).

Practically speaking, it is not wise of parents to wait for a child to show symptoms of problems. It is simply good health practice to have a child's vision examined by a behavioral optometrist before age three and again before the child enters school and annually thereafter until adulthood. If this were done, we would find fewer students with learning difficulties and more adults with happier and more productive lives.

*Let us repeat a warning.* Checking a child's visual acuity on the time-honored Snellen eye chart—we are all familiar with this chart from our school days—is not enough. Nor is it enough to determine that the eyes are healthy.

## The Vision Examination

When a behavioral optometrist examines a patient's vision system, it is neither uncomfortable nor demanding of the patient. Properly prepared for it, a youngster can find it interesting, even fun.

A thorough examination takes from 30 to 60 minutes on the first visit and includes a battery of tests (many of which are like playing games). Specific tests given will vary with each child's individual needs. In addition to the review of the child's health history and an examination to confirm the physical health of the eyes, the vision examination by the behavioral optometrist typically includes:

- tests of the ability to see sharply and clearly at near and far distances;
- tests to determine nearsightedness, farsightedness and astigmatism (refractive status) and the ability to maintain and change focus (accommodative status);
- a test of eye coordination to be certain the eyes work as a team (binocularity) at both near and far distance;
- a test to determine if the child is not using one eye;
- a test of depth perception;
- motor tests of gross and fine motor ability;
- tests to determine visual-perceptual and visual information processing ability.

All the results of the various tests of visual functioning are then compared to expected developmental levels. Where results fall below expected levels, optometric vision therapy may be recommended and this may include several courses of action.

## Vision Care: Lenses, Therapy or Both?

If the examination by the practitioner of optometric vision therapy reveals evidence of vision imbalances, lenses may be prescribed. Vision therapy may also be suggested. When lenses and therapy are used together, the benefits of each are increased.

**Lenses**—Often, particularly when vision imbalances are minor, lenses are needed only for schoolwork; this is to take the stress off the vision system. Optometrists who specialize in vision therapy base their lens prescriptions on concepts different from those used by general optometrists and ophthalmologists.

In general, the latter two groups use lenses only in one way. They prescribe *"compensating"* lenses, which treat symptoms, not causes.

For instance, if a child is nearsighted—commonly a symptom of a vision imbalance—compensating lenses can provide 20/20 eyesight. Bur as the imbalance increases, as it almost always does, stronger and stronger lenses usually have to be prescribed to maintain 20/20 sight because the vision imbalance is still there.

Since this approach is sight-oriented, the underlying causes of the nearsightedness (or whatever the symptom) are not being treated. The vision system is not being brought into balance. If it were, the need for these compensating lenses might well be eliminated.

The optometrist who specializes in vision therapy uses lenses in various ways:

**Preventive lenses**—to prevent a problem in the vision system of someone diagnosed "at risk";

**Developmental lenses**—to support and nurture an immature vision system while helping it develop normally; also to help the vision system cope with visual stress;

**Remedial lenses**—for a specific problem, such as an inability to sustain focusing, until that ability has developed.

**Optometric Vision Therapy**—This involves an array of procedures designed to achieve or maintain an optimally balanced and flexibly functioning vision system. It aims to teach the entire vision system to operate at peak efficiency. A program tailored specifically by the behavioral optometrist to the individual patient can:

- help prevent the development of some vision problems such as myopia;
- aid in the correct development of vision abilities;
- enhance the efficiency and comfort of vision functioning;
- help cure and/or correct existing vision problems.

## Good Vision Is Learned, Not Inborn

The ability to see and correctly interpret what is seen does not appear automatically at birth. It develops over a lifetime and is shaped by one's experience and environment. The cornerstone of optometric vision therapy is the fact that vision is learned.

Care for Your Vision

Some children skip steps in their vision development, sometimes because of illness. Others may not be exposed to the necessary visual experiences or learning opportunities to develop their vision skills adequately,

Today's lifestyles put endless stresses on the vision systems of children and adults. Most of us use computers, video games and cell phones regularly, then add a few hours of TV viewing. The impact of these activities is a complication yet to be fully understood in terms of vision development. The school-age child is confronted by the tasks of reading and writing and other close work repeatedly interrupted by demands to shift focus to a teacher or the computer monitor. Lengthy staring into a display terminal screen may cause the individual to start having difficulty changing focus. These and other stresses can trigger or worsen a variety of vision imbalances. Eyes may lose their ability to "team." The farsighted and near-sighted individuals may become more so. And so on.

A program of optometric vision therapy can protect and repair the system. What the behavioral optometrist does is consider the various components of the process of vision.

Any problem areas are treated by reeducating, reinforcing or developing specific vision skills such as:

- clearness of vision at near and far distances;
- eye movement skills;
- eye focusing skills;
- eye aiming skills;
- eye-hand coordination;
- visual perception, identification and memory.

You may consider that all these skills are your natural inheritance. The fact is, from infancy, they must all be enhanced through experience and learning. Most people use their vision skills well enough to get along (but often, not as well as they might). A substantial percentage of the population does not learn one or another of these skills. Worse, they are deficient in a significant number of them.

This is where optometric vision therapy comes in. The behavioral optometrist prescribes a program of visual activities which will be performed in the optometrist's office, although many may also be assigned as home therapy.

The activities vary widely, depending on the individual's special needs. Some, like walking on a balance beam or jumping on a trampoline, will seem like play to a child. Others make use of equipment that is space age in its sophistication. The repetition of these visual activities is aimed at improving vision by improving the integration of all the sensory motor activities with vision at the helm. The therapy works to enhance visual monitoring ability, visualization skills and visual perceptual abilities, among others. The following case histories show that vision is learned.

## The Surprising Case of Michael May

When he was three, Michael May was blinded in a chemical explosion. This didn't stop him! It definitely didn't slow him down. May became a three-time Paralympics Gold Medalist and a world record holder in downhill speed skiing. He managed a full family and business life equally well. The amazing story of his life is told in the 2007 book, *Crashing Through – A True Story of Risk, Adventure, and the Man Who Dared to See,* by Robert Karson.

The book relates how, as an adult, May had a corneal transplant. In contrast to several unsuccessful transplants when he was a youngster, this surgery was successful. Two months after the procedure, however, the ophthalmologist was puzzled at May's inability to see clearly. Although May's eye and optics were near perfect, his visual acuity was poor. As far as the doctor was concerned, by now, May ought to be able to drive.

"The issue must be your visual cortex, your brain," the surgeon told May.

How true! Research scientists Professor Donald MacLeod and Dr. Ione Fine were fascinated by May's situation, involved as they were in studying the effects of long-term visual deprivation. Study Michael May they did. In fact, after she published a paper on May in 2003, in the journal, *Nature Neuroscience* (Vol.6, #9), Dr. Fine received a 5-year grant to study long-term visual deprivation and sight recovery, as well as a professorship in the Department of Ophthalmology at the University of Southern California.

Sadly, May did not seek the services of an optometrist specializing in vision therapy. He managed to develop his own coping strategies but it's tantalizing to wonder what help he might have received from a practitioner in a profession that for many decades has helped individuals learn to develop their vision, whatever the challenge, as you can read in the section at the end of this chapter about NORA, an organization that works across disciplines.

## Legally Blind at Fifteen

Angela was 27 years old when she was referred to Dr. Michele Hlava in Somerset West, South Africa. Legally blind (which is 20/200), she had her own guide dog, named Aggie. Angela was born prematurely at 27 weeks; a twin, but not identical (her brother has sufficient sight so that as an adult he is able to drive). Angela was on oxygen at birth for some 2-3 months but the oxygen content was not correct; the optic nerve of the right eye was affected and that of the left eye more severely damaged. Angela had no sight at all in her left eye, and visual acuity of some 20/400 in her right eye. However, at the age of 15, she lost all the sight in her right eye. The cataracts that developed were not removed until 2006, when Angela was 27.

Like many others who have been told that it is pointless to search for help, in this young woman's case, the comment by a medical specialist, was, "Why waste medical insurance money by inserting intraocular lenses because she will never see.'" Fortunately, Angela heard through the grapevine that Dr. Hlava worked with victims of traumatic brain injury and she decided to ask for help. This required some planning: a friend walked Angela and her guide dog, Aggie, past Dr. Hlava's office the day before the appointment to teach Aggie the route. The next day, Aggie brought Angela to the office.

Dr. Michele Hlava made no promises and began by starting Angela on wearing contact lenses; she had the young woman come in every few days so that the lenses could be cleaned and changed. Optometric vision therapy was also begun. Dr. Hlava explained to Angela, "We are literally teaching you to see." Neurobiofeedback therapy was also begun, with Dr. Donovan Savage. After 6 months of optometric vision therapy and neurobiofeedback therapy, Angela's right eye began to straighten. Thanks to the vision therapy, there was a considerable reduction in her nystagmus (in general terms, this is a constant twitch— technically it is known as an involuntary rapid, repetitive movement of an eye, horizontal, vertical, rotatory or mixed). Angela's left eye was mostly in an upward, out-turned gaze and still slightly nystagmic.

At this point, Dr. Hlava decided to request that intraocular lenses be inserted. This would require surgery by an ophthalmologist. When the medical specialist examined Angela, he was surprised that Angela could distinguish light from dark and shadow in light. He was also astonished at the reduction in Angela's twitch, or nystagmus, and the improvement in her vergence ability.

The surgery was successful, although optometric vision therapy and neurofeedback therapy needed to be continued. By now, Angela had peripheral vision and could see, albeit in a somewhat blurred way, from her side to about half way towards the center of her stomach in a circular area (some 180 degrees to about 155 degrees). Her vergence improved daily; the twitch in the right eye was greatly reduced but her left eye tended to drift out when she was tired. Although Angela will never have 20/20, or even 20/60, the use of her peripheral vision is a great asset in her life, a dramatic change from being legally blind.

How has this amazing improvement in her vision affected Angela's life? She is happier! She also has a boyfriend. As for Aggie, the guide dog, she has to go to "guide dog school" from time to time, because she is fast becoming Angela's pet.

## The Neuro-Optometric Rehabilitation Association International (NORA)

A multidisciplinary organization, NORA was established in 1989 to provide and advocate for vision rehabilitation/habilitation of individuals through the understanding and applications of the current principles in vision science. The visual system is really a relationship of sensory-motor functions which are controlled and organized in the brain. Some 70 percent of all sensory input fibers to the brain begin in the eye, more than twice the neural input of all the other senses combined. The visual system is represented in every major lobe of the brain, as well as the midbrain and brainstem. Therefore, neurological compromise, whether acquired (e.g. Down's syndrome or cerebral palsy), or degenerative (e.g. Parkinson's disease or multiple sclerosis), frequently affects the visual system. NORA members are rehabilitation professionals, educators, neurologically challenged patients, brain-injury survivors and family members.

What these NORA members have in common is a mutual intention to advance the art and science of visual rehabilitation/habilitation of the neurologically challenged population. The emphasis in the association is on professional education and dissemination of existing technologies to address the frequently neglected visual-motor and visual-perceptual components of dysfunction in the neurologically affected person.

**4**

# Vision Skills and Challenges

**M**any different visual skills are involved in a child's learning to cope with living in the complicated, ever-changing dynamics of family and school life. Young children must learn to understand what's going on around them so that they can understand where they fit into things. Clear sight is not sufficient. Perception then interpretation are the keys to understanding and vision plays a role in each of these. If children have difficulty learning to read, later they will have serious challenges trying to read to learn.

We're probably all familiar with the vision skills listed below, but we may not realize how vital they are if youngsters are to succeed in school and in life. Fortunately, all of these skills can normally be developed or improved through optometric vision care.

1. **Clearness of Vision (Acuity)** – the ability to see clearly at near and far distances. Clarity at distance is about the only skill tested by the usual eye chart exam, the Snellen eye chart exam that tells you that you have 20/20 acuity or you don't. Generally, children who have poor distance acuity are nearsighted. They may do well at reading, less well at sports. The farsighted child tends to have more difficulty reading but, often, does better at sports than the nearsighted youngster.

2. **Eye Movement Skills (Fixation Ability)** – the ability to point the eyes accurately at an object and keep the eyes on the target, whether the object is moving or stationary. Without good eye movement skills you can't clearly follow a moving object, such as a ball in flight. You can't move your eyes smoothly across a line of text on a page or on the computer screen. A child can't shift the eyes from a close object to a far one.

Vision Skills & Challenges

3. **Eye Focusing Skills (Accommodation)** – the ability to adjust the focus of the eyes as the distance from the object varies. Most children are capable of a large amount of change of focus but fine, accurate controls breaks down more easily under stress. Excellent eye focusing is a skill common to superior athletes.

4. **Eye Aiming Skills (Converging and Diverging)** – the ability to turn the eyes inward or outward when looking from objects close up to objects far away and back again. These skills must be closely coordinated with eye focusing skills. Inadequacies in these areas seriously hamper reading ability and athletic performance.

5. **Eye Teaming Skills (Binocular Fusion)** – the ability to coordinate and align the eyes precisely so that the brain can fuse the input it receives from each eye. Even a slight misalignment can cause double vision, which in turn the brain may try to eliminate by suppressing the use of one eye. In one way or another, the brain will react in a disturbed and defensive manner to confusing signals from the eyes.

6. **Eye-hand Coordination** – the ability of the vision system (eye-brain connection) to coordinate the information received through the eyes in order to monitor and direct the hands. This skill is important for learning to write (poor handwriting is often related to poor eye-hand coordination). This ability is essential to good performance in most sports.

7. **Visual Form Perception** – the ability to organize images on the printed page into letters and/or words. It is one of the most important skills used in learning to read and is developed through both experience and practice.

8. **Auditory-Visual Coordination** – the ability to integrate auditory and visual coordination develops as a child grows. When there are problems with auditory-visual integration, it may show as slow reading and difficulty with spelling and with sound-symbol associations.

## "My Hands Won't Do What I See!"

**Dan** was 12 years old when he was referred to Dr. Earl Lizotte (Massachusetts) by his school's Special Ed teacher because Dan complained he couldn't make his hands do what he saw. This is known as a perceptual-motor disability.

The visual exam showed that Dan had never learned the skill of making smooth eye movements. Instead, he often preferred to track with gross head movements—this uses large neck muscles rather than the much smaller eye movement muscles (oculo-motor dysfunction). The youngster also had eye-hand coordination problems.

After 15 weekly visits for vision therapy and work at home, Dan was functioning normally in school and continued to work with Special Ed to catch up on work that he had missed.

## Basic Conditions of Risk

**Eye Disease**   The American Optometric Association (AOA) tells us that school-age children rarely have serious eye disease. But AOA explains that two types of minor eye infections—blepharitis and sties—may be indications of imbalances in the vision system. (Blepharitis is an inflammation of the eyelids, which sometimes can be identified by yellowish crusts at the base of the eyelashes.)

**Nearsightedness**   What the eye doctor calls "myopia" is commonly called nearsightedness. The AOA tells us that "nearsightedness is the only refractive vision condition that increases significantly in incidence throughout the school years." You can expect to find it in a small percent of children between five and nine years of age. It increases in incidence, often doubling among children ten to twelve and continues to rise along with the years of school experience. It's something to be on the lookout for.

Nearsighted individuals can see clearly up close but not at a distance. Watch students for these signs:

- a tendency to hold their books closer to their eyes than is normal;
- bending their heads down close to the page when they write;

- twisting their faces into a squint when they are trying to see the chalkboard.

**Myopia—Preventive Treatment**   The quick fix most often used for nearsightedness is prescription lenses. These can compensate for and provide good visual acuity. The problem is that these "compensating" lenses usually need periodic changing and strengthening because myopia is usually progressive.

A more specialized and, in the long run, a more rewarding approach to nearsightedness is the preventive treatment of optometric vision therapy. This care takes the form of "learning" lenses (in contrast to "compensating" lenses) and vision therapy. Similarly, these and other special methodologies are also used to slow or stop the progression of nearsightedness (myopia control).

Nature designed human eyes primarily for sharp, clear seeing at a distance, the eyes of the hunter, the farmer, the sailor at sea. Our eyes were not designed for the endless stresses put upon them by modern living with our books, television viewing, computer screens, video games and cell phones. Even high-speed travel exacts a toll on vision.

**Today, doctors of optometry who practice vision therapy can often prevent, reduce or control the myopia caused by environmental stresses by prescribing "learning" lenses. This type of lens has a mild prescription that reduces the amount of stress on the vision system. Usually, such learning lenses are necessary only for reading and close work.**

A number of doctors of optometry, including Drs. M. Albalas, Yves Bastien, Steve Gallop, Jacob Liberman and Cliff Fukushima, have written about their success in reducing, sometimes eliminating their own nearsightedness through optometric vision therapy.

**Farsightedness**   This is technically known as "hyperopia." The AOA tells us that most school-age children are farsighted—as nature intended them to be. They can usually see well at both distance and near; but there is a drawback. In most cases, farsighted children have to exert extra effort to bring their vision into sharp, clear focus for both far and near seeing.

For most such children, this presents no problem. But a small percent of children aged five to twelve have high degrees of farsightedness and need help to relieve the tension of focusing, especially when using their eyes for close work.

Again, most routine school eye chart examinations will not catch such problems. It's up to the parents and teachers to recognize the signs. Symptoms of hyperopia include:

- difficulty in concentrating and maintaining a clear focus when reading or doing close work;
- eye or body tension when doing such work;
- muscle fatigue, headaches, nausea, aching or burning eyes after doing close work;
- poor reading ability;
- irritability or nervousness after sustained close-work concentration.

**Astigmatism**   This is the development of unequal curvature of the cornea, the clear, shiny part at the front of the eye. Thus, the light gathered in by the eye is not focused properly. The end result is blurred sight. The AOA notes that a low percent of school-age children have significant amounts of astigmatism. However, this represents an increase from that found in preschoolers. The symptoms of astigmatism are similar to those for other vision disorders and they call for the same action: a thorough vision examination by an optometrist who practices behavioral optometry.

**Crossed Eyes (Strabismus) and Lazy Eyes**   Crossed eyes and lazy eyes are two conditions that, while not common, put particular pressures on those who suffer from them. Crossed eyes is a condition in which the two eyes do not work together; one eye or the other may turn inward, outward, upward or downward, either all or some of the time. The causes are different. But the result is poor eye control. Ophthalmologists tend to blame poor eye control on the muscles of the eye and all too frequently advise surgery. The behavioral optometrist believes differently and has a less radical, more promising approach.

The condition of strabismus occurs because the individual's vision system has not learned to make the two eyes work together as a team. In rare cases, paralyzed of partially paralyzed muscles may indeed cause lazy eye, but such paralysis occurs in a relatively small percentage of the population.

It is not unusual, during the first five or six months, for an infant's eyes to appear crossed or unaligned for brief moments while the infant is learning to use the eyes together as a team. But, if by the age of 3 ½ months, the misalignment appears to be frequent or long-lasting, or is always with the same eye, it is wise to visit a practitioner of optometric vision therapy.

Crossed eyes can also develop at a later stage, as children reach school age. Oddly enough, the development is often so gradual that parents fail to recognize it. They get used to the child's appearance and it seems normal. In this case, the problem may be noticed first by the family doctor or at school.

**Crossed Eyes: A Cosmetic and Functional Problem**  Two major factors are involved in crossed eyes. One, the most obvious, is appearance. Crossed eyes look funny, peculiar, different. And "different" is the last thing your school-age child wants to be. Two, because of the "difference," crossed eyes can inhibit a child's emotional and social development. They can also cause personality problems by isolating the individual from other youngsters and giving the child a poor self-image.

*A child rarely outgrows crossed eyes.* Therefore, parents are wise to seek help as soon as they spot the symptoms.

## What Are the Treatment Choices?

For several decades, the conventional medical treatment for crossed eyes has been surgery. Today, however, the specialists in behavioral optometry recommend *against surgery* particularly in cases where their examinations show obvious vision imbalance.

The reasons are several. First, surgery usually does not offer a permanent solution to the problem, as you can read in Chapter 6, about "Stereo Sue." In surgery, the eye muscles are cut so that the eyes look straight (if the surgeon has judged it to the precise degree).

However, *since no effort is made to teach the eyes to work together as a team,* the underlying imbalance remains and there is a strong tendency for the eyes to turn again. In many cases, repeated operations are necessary, yet there's no guarantee of total success.

In contrast, optometric vision therapy has a greater success rate particularly in treating crossed or out-turning eyes than surgery. In fact, because it treats the underlying cause, optometric vision therapy may be able to solve the problem because once the eyes learn how to work together as a team, there is less of a tendency for them to turn.

## Lazy Eye, Not Lazy Child

**Amblyopia** is often called "lazy eye" and it is a condition in which clear, sharp sight in one eye is lowered or apparently lost and cannot be improved with prescription "compensating" lenses. It affects about 2% of children.

The AOA tells us that there are different kinds of lazy eye. The most common type is a side effect or complication stemming from crossed eyes or from a vision condition in which one eye is much more nearsighted or farsighted than the other. In either of those situations, the two eyes send separate and different messages to the brain, which is not able to integrate them. Therefore, the brain often turns off the message from one eye. Since the ability to see sharply and clearly is a learned skill, central visual acuity never develops properly in the eye that the brain has turned off.

The one-eyed vision that results can affect other vision skills, such as the ability to judge distances, although a youngster with a lazy eye will not realize this. Once again, it is left to parents and teachers to identify the condition.

Look for the child who noticeably favors one eye (head-tilting is one clue) or who has a tendency to bump into objects. Since poor vision in one eye does not necessarily mean amblyopia or lazy eye (it could be nearsightedness), amblyopia can only be definitely diagnosed by a professional examination. Remember that the lazy-eyed child can become one-sided in responses and movements and may not develop the concept of opposites; perhaps there will be difficulty in balancing and in sports.

**Practitioners of optometric vision therapy believe that near and farsightedness and astigmatism are adaptations individuals make so that they can perform well. The need for such adaptations may be alleviated when the entire vision system is brought into balance.**

## How Optometric Vision Therapy Helps

This therapy works with the visual perceptual system and the various subsystems that integrate with vision. The pathways of the vision system include neuromuscular, neurophysiological and neurosensory systems. The eyes are the external receptors for the vision system. Light (radiant energy) is converted at the retinal level into electrical energy. This energy follows the visual pathways to the visual cortex. Developmental gaps, lags, warps or distortions at any point along the way will disrupt the efficiency of the system. Optometric vision therapy is often able to:

- Prevent or modify vision imbalances such as nearsightedness (myopia) and astigmatism;

- Develop the visual abilities and skills needed to achieve at school, work and sports;

- Reduce or eliminate chronic health problems, including travel sickness, bed-wetting, headaches, migraines, tension, teeth-grinding, light sensitivity, muscle pain, depression, alcoholism and schizophrenia.

## Computers, iPods, Hand-held Video Games and Cell Phones

The screens used on computers and devices like iPods, video games and cell phones continue to be sources of vision complaints, according to the Optometric Extension Program Foundation (OEPF). A non-profit foundation, OEPF has devoted decades to providing postdoctoral behavioral optometric education and publishing related journals, papers and books for professionals and the general public as well as arranging conferences around the world.

The screens used with today's technology have smoothed away the blurry images and small-area flicker we used to experience. This doesn't mean we're not continuing to assault our vision as we stare at the computer or device of choice. The whole issue of having to force your eyes to focus on small images for long periods is extremely fatiguing. Part of the problem is that the high-definition screens encourage us to look at them for longer periods. We forget to look away often enough. Irritated eyes, burning eyes, blurred vision and eyestrain are still the norm. Physical complaints are related, also, from headaches to aching necks, backs, shoulders and hands.

Anyone who uses contemporary video devices and computers a lot will have measurable fatigue in the eye accommodation mechanism, as well as an increased blink rate. Constant, close-range viewing of screens requires precise teaming of the eyes for sustained periods.

Visual stress leads to lowered performance. Children (adults, too) react to stress by avoiding work, or else they work under stress with lowered comprehension. In some cases, they adapt to stress by becoming nearsighted or suppressing the use of one eye.

Adults must be alert for the symptoms of visual problems, especially among youngsters who are now exposed to lengthy use of computers, video devices and cell phones.

# 5

# An Epidemic of Developmental Disabilities?
## Autism Spectrum Disorders (ASD)
## Attention Deficit Disorder (ADD)
## Attention Deficit/Hyperactivity Disorder (AD/HD)

The Centers for Disease Control and Prevention (CDC) explained in 2007 that disorders in the autism spectrum (ASD) are the second most common serious developmental disability. More prevalent are speech and language impairments, learning disabilities and attention deficit/hyperactivity disorders (AD/HD). Data released by the CDC's Autism and Developmental Disabilities Monitoring Network found that about 1 in 150 children aged 8 suffer from autism spectrum disorders.

The Mayo Clinic website notes that ASD problems appear in early childhood, usually before the age of three. Though symptoms and severity vary, all autism disorders affect a child's ability to communicate and interact with others and are four times more severe in boys than in girls. Children usually have problems in three crucial areas of development: social interaction, language and behavior. Naturally, each child may have a unique pattern of behavior.

Although there is not a full population count of all individuals in the U.S. with an ASD, given their data on prevalence, the CDC estimated in 2007 that if 4 million children are born in the U.S. every year and the prevalence rate has been constant over the past two decades, it may be that an ASD will affect up to 560,000 individuals between the ages of birth to 21. The experts are in general agreement that back in the 1970s, the rate was lower. Arguments aside about the causes and whether this increase reflects better record keeping, more and more patients are appearing in optometric offices across the country.

In case after case, optometric vision therapy proves helpful with the serious developmental challenges in the autism spectrum.

## Three Valuable Books

Parents and educators caring for children with ASD—as well as adults dealing with their own ASD—will find the following three books of immeasurable help. *Envisioning a Bright Future, Interventions that Work for Children and Adults with Autism Spectrum Disorders* is the most comprehensive book on autism treatment presently available. It offers an unparalleled gathering of individual chapters by twenty informed authors whose expertise covers the spectrum of professionals caring for those with autism. In her Foreword, the Editor, Patricia S. Lemer, M.Ed., NCC, describes her work as an advocate for children with autism and related disorders and why she is especially interested in the role of vision and visual dysfunction in autism spectrum disorders.

A nationally certified counselor and co-founder and Executive Director of Developmental Delay Resources, Patricia Lemer's counseling work led her to interact with optometrists. The bridge she created between the worlds of psychology, education and optometry was extended when Robert Williams, the Executive Director of the OEP Foundation, suggested her role be strengthened. This meant attending conferences on learning disabilities and occupational therapy as a spokesperson for optometry and becoming Program Chair for the Washington Independent Services and Educational Resources. She also authored a pamphlet, "Attention Deficits: A Developmental Approach." In that pamphlet, Patricia Lemer explained that youngsters with allergies/nutritional deficits, sensory integration issues and those with vision issues all could be misdiagnosed as having ADD. Patricia Lemer has also written five articles for the *Journal of Behavioral Optometry*, three of which have won awards from the Optometric Editors Association.

The second significant book is *Seeing Through New Eyes: Changing the Lives of Children with Autism, Asperger Syndrome and Other Developmental Disabilities Through Vision Therapy,* by Dr. Melvin Kaplan of New York. This discusses the connection between vision and the behaviors in question as well as clarifying visual dysfunction

Developmental Disabilities?

and the role of optometric vision therapy (Dr. Kaplan also authored a chapter in *Envisioning a Bright Future*).

## Diagnosed Autistic: Jimmy, a 6-year-old

When Dr. Kaplan started optometric vision therapy with Jimmy, he found that the boy had no trouble with television viewing or balance board tasks. Yet when Jimmy was asked to balance on one foot while looking at himself in a mirror, he could not keep his balance. These and other observations give Dr. Kaplan valuable clues to the boy's visual style and paved the way for appropriate, helpful treatment.

When autistic children pinch or slap themselves, Dr. Kaplan explains that they do so because they desperately need a form of sensory data that their brains can process in order to "find" themselves in space. While behavior modification can help reduce these actions, which range from rocking to spinning and include unusual sensitivity to light, sound and touch despite being oblivious to pain, it makes far more sense to understand them and to correct the underlying visual dysfunction that creates the behaviors in the first place.

The Director of the Center for Visual Management in New York, Dr. Kaplan explains in his book how one autistic boy had an inability to pay attention to "self" and "space" at the same time.

## Ed's Flapping Hands

Ed, a ten-year-old autistic boy walked around Dr. Kaplan's training room before the testing, inspecting the place. The minute his eyes caught sight of himself in the full-length mirror, the boy's arms went up and he started to flap his hands. This was boy's solution to his difficulty with "self" and "space"—flapping his hands to inform his brain that he had a body.

Dr. Kaplan casually placed a beanbag on the boy's head, thus giving the youngster feedback about where his body was in space. This extra piece of information about his orientation freed the boy from the need to continually "find" himself and he responded by lowering his arms to his sides and standing normally.

A third invaluable book for parents, educators and others searching for answers on how to care for anyone diagnosed in the spectrum of attention-deficit/hyperactivity disorder (AD/HD), is *Without Ritalin, A Natural Approach to ADD,* by Dr. Samuel Berne, a behavioral optometrist in New Mexico (he also authored a chapter in *Envisioning a Bright Future*). *Without Ritalin* explores the unique route from vision anomalies in children to a diagnosis of AD/HD—and on to the subsequent overuse of Ritalin for all manner of learning and behavioral problems. Dr. Berne points out that in 2000, some 11.4 million Americans—mostly school-age boys—were given the drug Ritalin to help improve concentration. This meant that Americans were using five times as much Ritalin as the rest of the world.

A founding member of the Parcells Center for Personal Transformation, Dr. Berne began his study into the links between vision and attention disorders twenty years ago at the Gesell Institute at Yale University in Connecticut. In his book, which offers methods of treatment for AD/HD without the side effects of either stimulant or antidepressant drug therapies, you will discover information on:

- the latest research about AD/HD, including common physical, performance and attention cues;

- the relationship between vision disorders—such as the physical inability to keep both eyes pointed and focused at a near target (convergence insufficiency)—and AD/HD;

- the stages of normal behavioral development;

- analysis of the most commonly prescribed behavior-modification drugs, including psychostimulants (such as Ritalin, Cylert, Dexedrine, and ADDerol), antihypertensives (such as Clonodine and Tenex), anticonvulsives and antipsychotics.

Dr. Berne quotes Drs. I. Schwartz and A. Shapiro, editors of *The Collected Works of Lawrence W. Macdonald, O.D.,* Vol. 2, 1968-1979, p. 44, "Educational psychologists have found that 70 to 90 percent of all learning in school comes through the eyes." This is vision. He also draws from the book, *Vision: Its Development in Infant and Child,* by Arnold Gesell, Francis Ilg and Glenna Bullis, in which Arnold Gesell, M.D., a child development expert, said: "So interfused are vision and the action system that the two must be regarded as inseparable. To understand vision, we must know

Developmental Disabilities?

the child; to understand the child, we must know the nature of his vision."

In his book's Introduction, Dr. Berne explains why he incorporates a wide range of treatments for the patients with ADD and AD/HD he has treated (over 5,000) and who have, without exception, benefited significantly: "As I've helped AD/HD patients with their specifically vision-oriented problems (reading and writing, balance and coordination, for example) and learned more about AD/HD, I've seen how drug therapies simply are not helping. And so I've researched the conditions of my patients in depth and looked for an alternative, comprehensive and nontoxic treatment."

His DVD, "ADD to Autism: Reaching Your Child's Potential Naturally," explores the unique relationship between vision problems in children and the spectrum of disorders from autism to ADD. He demonstrates the Reflex Integration Program, a movement pattern regimen that helps children improve their ability to concentrate. This in turn helps improve their learning.

### The New England Adolescent Research Institute

This institute (NEARI), which was established in 1985, offers cutting-edge care for youths with complex learning disabilities at its day school in the Holyoke-Springfield area. Among the many specialists providing expert care for NEARI students is Dr. Earl Lizotte of Massachusetts, a behavioral optometrist. He has treated youngsters at the NEARI school and also at his office. Dr. Lizotte has seen teens labeled autistic and unable to read respond to optometric vision therapy. Not only have they been able, finally, to start on the process of learning to read, their classroom behavior has improved.

The team approach to helping vision, learning and behavior problems is usually necessary, as you can read in Chapter 9, "Repairing the Damage." Working on causes, not symptoms, is one thing. Repairing the damage is another. In addition to optometric vision therapy, a team may include experts in such fields as education, psychology, audiology, occupational therapy, nutrition and child development.

# 6

# It's Never Too Late

In the first decade of the 21$^{st}$ century, Dr. David Hubel, the 1981 Nobel Prize winner in Physiology/Medicine* offered this valuable advice to consumers seeking help:

**If an ophthalmologist or optometrist tells you this [that it's too late for the adult vision system to change] you should find somebody else.**

The fact that it is possible to make changes in adult vision was not news to optometrists who offer vision therapy to their patients. For decades, these optometric specialists had demonstrated that adults, as well as children of all ages, with vision problems could be helped by optometric vision therapy. However, Dr. Hubel's warning flew in the face of dogma that has believed, despite scientific evidence, that vision can be improved only up to a certain age, called a critical period.

## Stereo Sue

When Dr. Hubel made that statement, he was referring to the experience of Susan Barry, Ph.D., who was described as "Stereo Sue" in the *New Yorker* article of June 19, 2006, by Oliver Sacks, M.D. Stereo Sue had several eye surgeries as a child for an eye that turned in so that eventually her eyes were cosmetically straight. Yet, as the years went by, Sue, a college professor, had growing problems with her vision. She was forced to drive slowly and often lost her way. Her depth perception was poor and when reading she would lose her place or concentration. It was hard for Sue to focus on the letters on street signs or distinguish whether a person was walking towards or away from her.

---

\* Dr. Hubel shared the Nobel Prize with Drs. Roger W. Sperry and Torsten N. Wiesel for studies in the "functional architecture of the visual system."

Despite many eye exams, Sue was told her vision was adequate and nothing further could be done. Even when she began to see the world as "jittering." Optometrists understand that this happens when you are switching between the use of two misaligned eyes, as Sue was. Her eye doctors told Sue that she was too old to benefit from any form of vision therapy. "It would be a waste of time and money…simply too late," they said.

The 2007 pamphlet by the OEP Foundation, "The Story of Stereo Sue, Vision Therapy for the Adult," describes how "Sue discovered Dr. Theresa Ruggiero, an optometrist in Massachusetts who prescribed lenses designed to make it easier to use both eyes together as a team. Dr. Ruggiero also prescribed optometric vision therapy that helped Sue develop binocular vision. Sue Barry captured the imagination of scientists when she developed stereoscopic [3 dimensional or 3-D] vision at an age when many did not consider it possible."*

Visual skills can be improved throughout life. After optometric vision therapy, adults often have better:

- visual judgment when driving;
- accuracy and stability when looking from one place to another;
- depth perception or 3-D vision;
- visual processing speed and accuracy when reading or writing;
- comfort, stamina and productivity when using a computer.

## Helping People Around the World

Optometrists who offer vision therapy to their patients have case files filled with success stories similar to Stereo Sue's. Whether in Australia, New Zealand, South Africa, Japan, the U.K., or throughout Europe, youngsters and adults have been helped to overcome their vision problems. Often, because their vision imbalances had triggered learning, health and behavior issues, those difficulties had also been helped. Age is no deterrent to the help that vision therapy provides.

---

* Susan Barry's book, *Fixing My Gaze – A Scientist's Journey into Seeing in Three Dimensions*, was published in 2009 by Basic Books. It is available at www. oepf.org.

## Crippling Migraines

Rosemary B., of Sydney, Australia, had migraines most weeks. Little helped, even medication (Rosemary was also taking medication for high blood pressure). She had a severe reaction to glare and had to wear sunglasses as soon as she went outside. Even on overcast days, her reaction to glare was still so strong that she wore sunglasses. She went to Simon Grbevski,* a behavioral optometrist in Sydney, for help.

Reading glasses were prescribed and optometric vision therapy sessions of half an hour each. At session ten, halfway through the therapy, Rosemary realized she was driving to the optometrist's office without her sunglasses but feeling perfectly comfortable, even though it was a sunny day. Her reaction to glare had disappeared. Years later, Rosemary is still free of those crippling migraines.

## Too Late for These Teens?

**Suzie,** a 13-year-old girl, was referred to Dr. Earl Lizotte (Massachusetts) by a family friend. The year before, mother and daughter had been told that the girl would remain blind in her left eye for the rest of her life because it was too late for remediation.

The vision exam revealed that Suzie had a significant difference between the optics of the two eyes. One eye needed a weak lens for detailed work, while the other eye needed a strong prescription because it had to work so hard to see. The brain doesn't like to use too much energy; it prefers to conserve energy. In situations like Suzie's, the brain reduces the effort of the weak eye so that it won't compete with the strong eye. Gradually, this leads to a reduction of the weak eye's ability so it becomes a lazy eye (refractive amblyopia).

Suzie's visual acuity, or sight, with glasses, was 20/20 in one eye and 20/80 in the other. A special contact lens, a Toric, was prescribed for the left eye to help balance the focusing of the two eyes. After 48 weekly sessions of vision therapy, Suzie had 20/20 vision in each eye and her depth perception (stereopsis) was normal.

---

* Optometrists and dentists in Australia and the U.K. are not referred to as doctor.

**Richard B.**, a 13-year-old who was not able to read, went to Dr. Lizotte at his school's recommendation. The first visual exam revealed that his problem was quite severe. It was as if the boy had a Plexiglas barrier down the middle of his body that prevented the kind of smooth, normal movement from one side to the other, that happens when we move our eyes along a sentence while reading. This "barrier" develops when there have been delays in neurological development and skills do not develop. Gross muscles will be used, not fine motor muscles. Richard had what amounted to a jump in his mid-line crossing; the technical definition is a bilateral integrated developmental lag.

After 24 weekly sessions of vision therapy, Richard was not only reading, he was on the honor role at school.

## Frustration at Every Turn

**Gena and Bill L.** were concerned that their sons, aged eight and twelve, were only able to read three-letter words. At an evaluation by a special education consultant, the boys were given a specific test to see if optometric vision therapy would be helpful to them. Bill, who was watching carefully, suggested that Gena take the same test because her list of daily frustrations was astounding. Among other problems, she:

- could not back the car down the drive without running over the grass;
- could not pull the car into the garage straight;
- constantly bumped into people when shopping;
- frequently spilled food, so could not help serve meals at church.

Gena found the test tiring and the consultant advised Gena and her two sons to visit Dr. Christa Roser, an optometrist in Pennsylvania. At Dr. Roser's office, the visual analysis showed that Gena had poor eye teaming, poor eye movements and weak visual processing. Her peripheral vision was almost non-existent.

Gena and her two sons started optometric vision therapy, with regular office visits and activities at home. It took under three months of vision therapy for the boys but Gena needed almost nine months.

Over the years, an adult with vision imbalances develops coping mechanisms. While these may help manage daily routines, they are poor or inefficient visual habits. Optometric vision therapy helps replace bad habits with good ones and this takes time.

## Low Vision

The American Optometric Association (AOA) explains that the diagnosis of low vision is appropriate when a visual impairment is not fully treatable by medicine, surgery or conventional eyewear. Usually, we think of low vision being caused by problems such as macula degeneration, cataracts, glaucoma, retinal detachment and traumatic brain injury. Typically, we expect to find such problems in adults. However, low vision may affect young people also. For instance, premature infants and infants who have suffered strokes may have low vision. Each type of low vision problem requires a different therapeutic approach. You will find helpful information about how low vision can be helped on the AOA website (www.aoa. org/low-vision.xml).

It's Never Too Late

# 7

# Syntonic Optometry

The umbrella name of behavioral optometry shelters functional, developmental, pediatric, geriatric, sports and syntonic photo-optometry. If you haven't heard of syntonics—or the College of Syntonic Optometry—or come across *Light, Medicine of the Future*, the seminal book by Dr. Jacob Liberman, there's a culprit, an all too familiar one: sulfalinamide drugs. The advent of these drugs in the 1940s put syntonics on the back burner.

**Syntonics is optometric light therapy, a branch of eye care therapy conducted in clinical settings. Selected light frequencies are used by optometrists to treat a multitude of vision problems.**

Light therapy itself is hardly new. In 1903, the Nobel Prize in Physiology or Medicine was awarded to Niels Finsen, a Danish physician. His work in light therapy resulted in the healing of what had been considered an incurable disease, Lupis erithmatosis, a type of tuberculosis. Dr. Finsen's light therapy work also improved smallpox scarring. In the award ceremony, the Nobel Prize Committee said that Dr. Finsen had "opened a new avenue for medical science."

Dr. Finsen himself explained that during his work, he "encountered several effects of light. I then devised the treatment of smallpox in red light (1893) and further the treatment of lupus (1895)." Eventually, the Finsen Institute was opened and became the model for similar institutions in a number of countries. As a result, work with light therapy increased dramatically.

Researchers around the world wasted no time in exploring other possible applications of this phenomenal therapy. In the U.S., Dr. H. R. Spitler, who held both medical and optometric degrees, began studying the use of light therapy in 1909. His research and the clinical studies in the sanatorium that he directed validated the profound effect that light has on human function and health. His work became the basis of the clinical science of optometric light therapy, which Spitler named syntonics, from the word syntony, to be in agreement, in harmony, to bring into balance.

**The optometric therapy that developed as a result of Dr. Spitler's work physiologically helps integrate and balance our nervous system.**

**Optometrists have had great success using syntonics to treat children and adults with vision-related learning, reading and attention disabilities.**

**Individuals with crossed eyes and eye turns (strabismus), lazy eyes (amblyopia) and focusing and convergence problems are helped. So are those suffering from head trauma such as traumatic brain injury, stroke, retinal disease, headaches and senility.**

Jacob Liberman, O.D., Ph.D., wrote in *Light, Medicine of the Future*, "In 1923 and 1924, Spitler began a series of impressive experiments to evaluate the responses of different groups of rabbits living under different lighted environments.... Within three to eighteen months from the onset of the study, some startling results became apparent. The rabbits began to develop abnormal conditions such as the loss of fur (some total, some partial), toxic symptoms, abnormal body weight, digestive problems, sterility, abnormal bone development, and cataracts.

"...Recognizing that imbalances in both the autonomic nervous system and endocrine system were involved in the development of the abnormalities seen in these rabbits, Spitler further investigated how light might be affecting these systems. His research convinced him that the portions of the brain that directly control both the autonomic nervous system and the endocrine system receive input directly from the eyes (by the shortest, most direct, and most highly organized nerve pathways in the brain)."

Syntonic Optometry

The discoveries of his seventeen years of ongoing research were the foundation of the principles Spitler developed for what was then the new science of syntonics, and in 1933, he established the College of Syntonic Optometry (CSO) as a center for research and education. In his book, *The Syntonic Principle*, published in 1941, Spitler theorized that low-frequency light (red) stimulates the sympathetic branch of the autonomic nervous system and high frequency (blue) stimulates the parasympathetic branch. Of the 3,067 individuals he studied, 2,791 (90.7 per cent), responded positively to syntonics.

Optometric research published in the *New England Journal of Medicine* supports the theory that a timing problem (a temporal deficiency) exists in the brains of poor readers.* We now know that vision works as a dual pathway system. The fast-acting pathway is the transient portion of vision input that controls where to look. It is located in the retinal periphery rather than the central retina.

Poorly integrated timing (peripheral input) degrades central effectiveness and reduces visual information process so that reading loses fluency and meaning. Optometrists (not other vision professionals) who offer syntonics, measure the quality and size of peripheral awareness (this is visual field testing) in relation to reading disability. Visual fields are commonly diminished in children with learning and reading problems. After syntonic treatments, visual fields expand to normal and when they do, practitioners, patients, parents and teachers report measurable improvement in behavior, cognition, learning (reading) and self-esteem.

The need for successful ways to help children improve their reading and learning skills has increased awareness of optometric vision therapy as well as syntonic therapy. Acceptance has grown with the constant publication of the valuable clinical research that validates such health therapies.

Evidence of the effects of colored light on biological function was dramatically demonstrated by J. N. Ott in the 1970s. His book, *Health and Light* (Pocket Books, 1973) was followed by his paper in the *Journal of Biosocial Research* (#7, Part 1, 1975), "Color and

---

* "A defective visual pathway in children with reading disabilities," *New England Journal of Medicine*, 1993 (328) 14:989-96.

Light, Their Effects on Plants, Animals, and People," and a film, "Exploring the Spectrum." Research in the following decade found that nerve pathways from the eye lead to specific brain centers that control biological rhythms. The 1970s was also the time when the general public became aware of the beneficial effect of light stimulation on seasonal affective disorder (SAD).

**Light shone into the eyes is absorbed into the large supply of blood circulating behind the retina. Only in the eyes do all visible wavelengths have direct access to the blood.**

A decade after Dr. Ott's publications, clinical studies by Dr. R. M. Kaplan in the *International Journal of Biosocial Research* (1983;5(1)) and Dr. J. Liberman in the *Journal of Optometric Vision Development* (1986;17) clearly demonstrated that in students who had syntonic therapy, the usual result of this relatively short-term treatment is improvement in visual skills, peripheral vision, memory, behavior, mood, general performance and academics. Such studies confirmed that large numbers of children with learning problems have reduced sensitivity of their peripheral vision. During and after syntonics, the youngsters had improvements in peripheral vision and visual skills. Control subjects who did not receive the therapy showed no improvement in their peripheral vision, their symptoms or their academic and overall performance.

The College of Syntonic Optometry has become an international organization, providing basic and advanced education at its annual conferences on light and vision to optometrists and other professionals and in other conferences in the United States and around the world. The college's charter is to promote the therapeutic use of colored light in the clinical practice of optometrists through postgraduate education and research.

Ray Gottlieb, O.D., Ph.D., a behavioral optometrist in Rochester, New York, is also Dean of the College of Syntonic Optometry. He suggests that breakthroughs in science, technology and medicine in the 21st century will be about light and notes:

*Communications technology has already embraced the superior qualities of light over electricity in the move to fiber optic, optical readers and optical computers. Surgeons have* *discovered the superiority of the laser over the knife. Atoms and molecules can be altered, arranged and stored using light Atomic physicists now use laser-laser interactions to hold and examine single atoms. What a few years ago required miles of land area and billions of dollars can now be done on a desktop for $100,000.*

He adds that scientists have even created matter from the interaction of coherent light:

*In Russia, light therapy has been found to dramatically improve healing and reduce side effects in life-threatening diseases. Ultra-violet light injected into the lungs using needles and fiber optics has been found to be twice as effective as drug therapy in curing diphtheria and pulmonary tuberculosis if treated early.... Red light...heals intractable lesions such as stomach ulcers over 95% of the time without the use of antibiotics or other drugs. Chronic diabetic lesions are being treated by low powered laser stimulation.*

## Double Vision and Crossed Eyes

P.T., a 78-year-old woman, came to Dr. Gottlieb for help because she had double vision. Two months earlier, her eyes had suddenly crossed. Since the death of her husband, 10 months before, she had been mentally confused and emotionally distraught. An examination by her neurologist was inconclusive. After twelve 20-minute treatments [of syntonic optometry], her eyes straightened and she was coherent, having regained mental and emotional balance.

Dr. Gottlieb asked what the patient thought had helped her.

"The green light," she said. "Every time I watched the green light, I could feel waves and ripples inside my head. Finally, during one light session, I felt a kind of pop and everything became clear."

## An Undiagnosed Head Injury

L.T. was ten when her mother brought her to Dr. Gottlieb for an examination. She was concerned because her daughter had stopped riding her bicycle. The child was complaining that she couldn't see well enough. Her history revealed a recent head injury. Three months earlier the youngster had fallen down a flight of stairs and hit her head on the door jamb at the bottom of the stairs. She had not been examined by a doctor at that time. The visual exam showed two serious problems: the girl was seeing double and also had tunnel vision, that is, her range of vision was severely restricted. Such acute problems required the use of green/blue light therapy. When her progress was evaluated a week later, her vision was no longer restricted–indeed, it had returned to normal–and she was not seeing double.

## Brain Injury, Traumatic and Mild

Brain injury is one of the most common of all neurological disorders and unfortunately the most under-diagnosed. In 2006, the Centers for Disease Control (CDC) estimated that some 1.4 million people in the U.S. were in accidents that caused traumatic brain injury (TBI). Approximately 75 percent of the injuries reported were classified as mild. The truth is that these are low figures: only people hospitalized were counted. Individuals examined in emergency rooms and sent home, those who didn't go to the hospital but instead saw their own doctors and those without medical care were not counted. The CDC put the annual costs for such injuries at $60 billion in 2000. It's also estimated that at least 2 percent of the population in the U.S. is living with lasting disabilities that are the result of TBI. In essence, we have a minor epidemic of brain injury.

Dr. Gottlieb writes,

*The severity of the injury does not always predict the severity of symptoms. A seemingly minor injury can cause serious and lasting disability.... Disturbances still present at one year are at high risk of being permanent. Emotional and cognitive behaviors are especially vulnerable. Dizziness, headache, sensory hypersensitivity, impaired attention, poor memory, anxiety...can be more disabling at one year than just after the injury.*

*Even "fully recovered" patients may suffer from fatigue, cognitive dips, emotional swings or symptoms after modest alcohol consumption.... They typically complain that they lose things, have difficulty concentrating, forget what they are doing or saying, can't organize their environment or activi-*

*ties, and are overly irritable, depressed, nervous, discouraged or angry.*

*Many patients with post-concussion symptoms suffer without knowing the cause. Subtle changes may first appear many weeks post-trauma and gradually increase over months. Parents may become aware of changes in their child's behavior but not link them to last month's minor head bump. Adults might not suspect their headache, irritated mood, chronic fatigue, indecision, depression, reading difficulty or poor memory is due to a mild head injury. Caretakers may not attribute a sudden increase in Alzheimer's symptoms to a MTBI.* (See www.cdc.gov and search for mild traumatic brain injury, MTBI.)

## A Session of Optometric Color Vision Therapy

Usually, this type of therapy consists of a 20-minute light treatment, preferably 3 to 5 days a week. Eighteen treatments usually produce lasting recovery. Patients look into a syntonic instrument at a 2-inch diameter circle of filtered light located 20 inches away. If the symptoms, history and exam of the vision system suggest MTBI within the past 30 months, blue/green light treatments are prescribed. When conditions are more chronic, yellow/green light is used. Indigo treatments may be added for headache or pain reduction.

After seven treatments of optometric color therapy, syntonic protocol includes a careful progress evaluation of the individual's vision system, their symptoms and any other findings. Typically, at this point, findings include increased peripheral vision and a reduction in the patient's symptoms although recovery may not yet be total. This validates the therapy received up to that point. If little improvement is noted in the progress testing, this indicates that the color filter prescription should be modified and monitored with subsequent testing. Patients may be referred to their physicians for additional tests if the results are not positive at this stage. As a rule, after eighteen treatments, the vision is normal and problems, whether emotional, behavioral, visual or cognitive, have gone. Patients are happier, more social and manage their daily routine much more easily after syntonic treatment.

## Do Other Professionals Use Syntonics?

Since the 1990s, other professionals have joined the ranks of the College of Syntonic Optometry and explored wider clinical applications of light therapy. One of the best books for an overview of the different light therapies and light technologies now in current use is *Light Years Ahead*, edited by Brian Breiling. The North American Laser Therapy Association (NALTA) held its first conference in October 1999. The meeting was held collaboratively with the FDA to clarify regulations concerning laser photo-stimulation and laser acupuncture and to educate leaders of government organizations about clinical application of low-level laser therapy.

In the U.S., the currently preferred medical treatment for neonatal jaundice is the use of blue/green or blue light on the skin of newborns. Light therapy has been successfully used for preventing dental caries and stress-related heart and cerebrovascular disease, and for treating asthma, herpes simplex, rheumatoid arthritis, damaged nerves, tendons, muscles and bones, and for reducing infection, inflammation and tendonitis. It has also been applied in laboratory experiments and in clinics for relieving pain and stimulating immune function.

The Russians and researchers in former Eastern bloc countries have discovered that at certain wavelengths, within a limited low-intensity range, light stimulation increased the healing of infected or slow healing wounds. The International Society for Optical Engineering (SPIE) has sponsored several conferences on the effects of low-power light on biological systems (transcripts of those meetings and abstracts can be read on the SPIE web pages).

During the early part of the 20th century, as Dr. Spitler was developing syntonics, practitioners like Drs. Skeffington, Harmon, Renshaw and Getman were demonstrating that vision is learned and thus amenable to remediation. The work of these pioneering optometrists established the foundation of behavioral vision care and the practice of optometric vision therapy. By the 21st century, the specialty of behavioral optometry had grown to include sports, pediatric and geriatric care as well as syntonics.

At the time that this book was published, syntonic optometry was not as widely available as optometric vision therapy. Approximately one quarter of the optometrists around the world who offer optometric vision therapy incorporate syntonics in their practice (you can go to www.syntonicphototherapy.com to find a practitioner). Interest is increasing, as shown by the numbers of practitioners who take the introductory syntonics course at annual conventions. The field of photomedicine is also growing and the use of light as a health therapy is being researched by government agencies in the U.S. and elsewhere and various journals have published research articles.*

---

* *Science* and *Nature* have published articles such as "Therapeutic photobiomodulation for methanol-induced retinal toxicity," by J. T. Eells et al, from the proceedings of the National Academy of Sciences, PNAS, March 18, 2003, Vol. 100; 6: 3439-44. This research notes: "Low-energy photon irradiation by light in the far-red to near-IR spectral range (630-1,000 nm) with low energy lasers or LED arrays has been found to modulate various biological processes in cell culture and animal models. This phenomenon of photobiomodulation has been applied clinically in the treatment of soft tissue injuries and the acceleration of wound healing."

Research reported in the article, "High Sensitivity of Human Melatonin, Alertness, Thermoregulation, and Heart Rate to Short Wavelength Light," Christian Cajochen, et al. (*J. Clin Endocrinol Metab* 2005;90:1311-16, www.endo-society. org) noted: "Light can elicit acute physiological and alerting responses in humans...."

# 8

## Optometric Vision Therapy
## The Indisputable Proof of Research

The following statement may seem simple but it is a vital key to understanding why optometric vision therapy is a successful and valuable therapy.

**Vision is primarily a learned process that begins at birth. This is why, regardless of age, you can be helped to learn, relearn or reinforce specific vision skills.**

Joyful reports from parents about how their child was helped and enthusiastic comments from adults whose problems have been eliminated are not acceptable as definitive proof that optometric vision therapy is valid.

Reliable research is the traditional way that claims about any therapy are validated. Such research needs to be scientific, meticulously planned and carefully executed. You will find that optometric vision therapy has been validated by scrupulous research for decades. As for contemporary work, research in 2005 was funded by the National Eye Institute of the National Institutes of Health and conducted at six clinical sites, all of which were Colleges of Optometry. Interestingly, the results were published in the *Archives of Ophthalmology* (2005;123:14-24), rather than any of the optometric journals.

In his guest editorial in the *Journal of Behavioral Optometry* (2005;16:48), Dr. Leonard J. Press, a behavioral optometrist in New Jersey, wrote, "Within days of its being published, a local ophthalmologist put a copy in the mail to me, with a cover note simply saying, 'Very impressive.'" However, as Dr. Press explains, other practitioners took exception to the study, although their objections were neither accurate nor scientifically based.

A small selection from the wealth of reliable scientific studies that document the positive results and value of optometric vision therapy is in the Appendix, under Scientific Studies. More studies are available in a range of journals and online. The *Bibliography of Near Lenses and Vision Training Research* is a valuable document published by the OEP Foundation. It contains over 1,500 references in 64 categories related to the functional, developmental and behavioral aspects of optometric vision care from research that has been published in over 200 publications. These include the *New England Journal of Medicine,* the *British Journal of Ophthalmology*, the *Canadian Journal of Surgery*, the *Australian Orthoptic Journal*, the *Scandinavian Journal of Psychology* and the *South Africa Medical Journal.*

Unfortunately for consumers, myths persist about optometric vision therapy, one being that there is no research, another being that optometric research is not valid. If you are given such misinformation, even the tired canard that after a certain age your vision cannot change, remember the statement by Dr. David Hubel, a co-winner of the 1981 Nobel Prize in Physiology or Medicine: "If an ophthalmologist or optometrist tells you this [that the adult visual system does not have the ability to change] you should find somebody else."

A succinct article, "The Myth of Critical Periods," by Dr. Paul Harris (www.oepf.org/Articles/critical.pdf) describes how the initial concept of a critical period came from observations of young chickens and ducks. "Conventional wisdom in the fields of neurology and development has led to general acceptance of the fact that 'critical periods' exist in the development of certain aspects of the human visual process. However, as more understanding of the supporting physiology of the neural networks that comprise the brain emerges, the length of time that makes up critical period must be extended to coincide with the only true critical period there is—death."

Optometric vision therapy is successful because it is a health care structured to treat the root of vision imbalances, not just symptoms. Professional organizations like the American Optometric Association (www.aoa.org), the College of Optometrists in Vision Development (www.covd.org) and the OEP Foundation (www.oepf.org) explain that optometric vision therapy offers treatment programs designed to teach the entire vision system to operate at peak efficiency.

## Training for Athletes

Even top athletes who have superior vision systems have chosen optometric vision training to sharpen their skills. Quick reaction time, fast and accurate judgment of distances and objects in motion, sharp, clear images, the perception of the athlete's body attitude and its position in space related to other bodies and objects around it—all these are necessary for superior athletic performances. All depend on a good, balanced vision system. The New York Knicks, New York Islanders, New York Yankees, Kansas City Royals, Dallas Cowboys, Chicago Black Hawks and the San Francisco 49ers are among those who have used and benefited from optometric expertise.

**U.S. Olympic contenders and professional sports teams have all learned that behavior is reaction to information from the vision system.**

A cover story in the February 24, 2003, issue of *USA Today*, highlighted the work of Drs. Ronald Berger and Harry Wachs with the National Football League. These Maryland optometrists have been conducting optometric tests on professional football prospects being considered by the NFL since 1986. They evaluate players for vision, motor, mental motivation, aggressiveness, competitiveness, leadership and teamsmanship on and off the field. The general manager of the Houston Texans, Charley Casserly, thought the optometrists were so valuable and necessary that he brought the services of Drs. Berger and Wachs with him after moving from the Washington Redskins.

Val Skinner, a professional golfer, is very articulate about the way optometric vision therapy helped her improve her game. She went to see Dr. Sue Lowe, a behavioral optometrist in Laramie, Wyoming, at the suggestion of a friend. After two years of watching her game deteriorate, her reaction was, "Why not try optometric vision therapy?" Val was waking every morning with headaches and grinding her teeth.

When Dr. Lowe said that on a scale of one to ten, Val's vision rated a two, the golfer was amazed. But she committed to two months of intensive therapy and tangible proof came early when the headaches and teeth grinding disappeared. Val says she can't put a percentage on how the therapy helped her as an athlete but her golfing is far superior now and equally as important, optometric vision therapy helped her as an individual.

As for children who do poorly at sports, often they are simply victims of vision problems. Since this kind of failure can affect children's acceptance by their peers, it can warp relationships and lead to negative self-images. It may even lead to a lifetime avoidance of physical activity.

Why let it happen when help is so readily at hand?

## Recognition from Other Professions

Behavioral optometry is a specialty. In the United States, it is practiced by approximately 12 percent of the doctors of optometry, in other words, those who have pursued the necessary extra postdoctoral training. On the other hand, the average ophthalmologist, family doctor, pediatrician or child psychologist usually knows little or nothing about optometric vision therapy because their education has not included courses in it.

In contrast, those professionals who do know of and value the therapy have no hesitation in sharing their expertise in this matter. Allan Cott, M.D., a psychiatrist in New York City, wrote in his book, *Help for Your Learning Disabled Child*, that he usually has his patients include a vision examination by a behavioral optometrist in their initial testing. He writes:

> *An examination of a learning-disabled child without a consultation and treatment by a developmental optometrist is an incomplete examination and treatment.*

Dr. Cott also points out that a child with problems grows up to become an adult with problems. Pediatrician Morris Wessel, M.D., of Cheshire, Connecticut, also discussed the value of optometric vision therapy in his book, *Raising a Healthy Child*. In the foreword to *Your Child's Vision* (by Dr. R. Kavner, a New York behavioral optometrist) and in other material he has authored, as well as the book, *Rickie* (about his daughter), Fredrich Flach, M.D., a New York City psychiatrist, describes optometric vision therapy as a valid valuable health therapy. General practitioner Dorothy Linley, M.D., of Cheshire, Connecticut, suggests that material on optometric vision therapy needs to be part of "required medical reading," particularly for physicians dealing with problem children.

Be warned. You will find a number of otherwise reliable advisors pooh-poohing behavioral optometry. They haven't done their homework. Consider the fact, also, that behavioral optometrist play significant roles in police tests of drivers for DUI and drug use.

## How Optometrists Work With Police

Since 1970, the Connecticut State Police have used the programs developed for them by Dr. C. Forkiotis, a behavioral optometrist based in Connecticut. A consultant for the U.S. Department of Transportation Research Office and the National Health Traffic Safety Administration for drug-testing detection and the National Standardized Behavioral Sobriety tests Dr. Forkiotis presented expert witness courses to police training officers, state prosecuting attorneys and county attorneys around America from the 1980s until his retirement in the 2000s. Drs. E. R. Bertolli and R. Pannone continue the work initiated by Dr. Forkiotis at the Connecticut State Police Academy, with their regular lectures on the Medical Aspects of Horizontal Gaze Nystagmus for the Driving While Intoxicated courses.

Dr. Jack Richman, an optometrist in the Boston area, has been the medical consultant to the International Chiefs of Police, Highway Safety Committee, since 1999. He is responsible for reviewing and writing the procedures and manuals used nationwide by law enforcement officers for alcohol and drug-impaired driving.

**The Scientific Basis for Standardized Behavioral Sobriety Tests** (alcohol gaze nystagmus). Field tests the police use to determine whether drivers are under the influence of alcohol or drugs involve vision and the vision system. Until the development of this testing, such cases had often been thrown out of court for lack of evidence. The use of such tests was supported in a landmark U.S. court decision in 1985.  Experts such as Dr. Forkiotis have helped U.S. police learn to test suspicious drivers for nystagmoid oscillation, the uncontrolled, erratic eye movement that develops when alcohol or drugs are in one's body.  Such eye movements are clues from the vision system that optometric specialists are trained to analyze and treat.

## Vision Training for Police Recruits – The Eyeport

The equipment used in optometric vision therapy can be simple, like the Brock String, which consists of beads on a string (see Ch. 9) or it can be the latest in electronics, like the Eyeport.  In an article in the *Journal of Behavioral Optometry* (2006;17:78-92), Dr. J. Liberman reported on a successful pilot study of the use of the Eyeport vision training system to enhance the visual performance of police recruits. Dr. Liberman and co-author Lisa Horth, Ph.D., explain that "… effective and efficient vision is among the most important attributes for police officers because of its role in self-protection as well as protecting society at large."

Law enforcement is a highly stressful job where one continually faces the effects of murders, violent assaults, accidents and serious personal injury.  A number of visual skills must be functioning optimally to guarantee that a police officer's response is quick, accurate and appropriate, especially when it involves shooting.  After a 3-week training period, the 9 recruits in the study (7 men 2 women) showed significant improvement in visual attention for objects, speed and span of perception and marksmanship.

As a result of the pilot study, Dr. Liberman was asked to make two presentations, the first in early 2006 to the International Association of Directors of Law Enforcement Standards and Training. The second presentation, a few months later, was to the Washington Association of Sheriffs and Police Chiefs.  Next, a study was requested by the Washington State Criminal Justice Training Commission to assess the value of including the Eyeport in police recruit training programs.

As this book went to the printer, the results from this study were still being evaluated.  However, if the results are significant, it may open the door for vision training to become part of all police recruit training programs nationwide.

## Not a Magic Cure-all

A clarification here is useful. No single health therapy is the answer for everyone. We are all different, our individual needs are unique. Adults and youngsters have found that optometric vision therapy has been of great benefit to them when their difficulties, whether learning, behavior or health problems, were related to vision imbalances.

Professional athletes like Edgar Martinez of the Seattle Mariners and Greg Vaughn of the San Diego Padres have excellent vision systems but they value optometric vision therapy. Why? When they improved their visual performance, their athletic performance improved—and so too their life in general.

When someone with migraines or acquired or traumatic brain injury or persistent depression is helped by optometric vision therapy, it is because the vision imbalances underlying their problems are eased. By treating causes, behavioral optometry helps relieves symptoms. Although optometric vision therapy is not the answer to every difficulty, the simple fact is that we have everything to gain and nothing to lose by making use of a valid therapy.

# 9

# Repairing the Damage
# The Team Approach

**W**hen you help youngsters with learning or behavior difficulties develop efficient vision systems, that's usually only
the *first* step along the way to helping them develop fully productive lives. Frequently, these children have not developed skills in
reading and writing. Often, they are behind their grade level in most
studies. Good work and study habits are foreign to them. They may
also have mild to severe emotional problems, which may range from
feelings of unworthiness to rebellious rage.

Fixing the cause of all these problems is one thing. Repairing the
damage is another. Usually, the repairs call for a team approach.
In addition to the behavioral optometrist providing vision therapy,
a team can include experts in such fields as education, psychology,
nutrition and child development. Specialists like Patricia S. Lemer,
M.Ed., NCC, have written extensively on the all-important team
approach. She makes the important point that prioritizing therapies is useful *after* youngsters have had their vision problems helped
(Chapter 5 has details about the book for which she is the Editor).

Among those optometric practitioners who cast the net wide to
embrace many healing modalities is Dr. Samuel A. Berne (Chapter
5 has information on his DVD and book); in the latter he explores
the impact on vision, learning and behavior of food allergies and
food sensitivities and the side effects of commonly prescribed medication). In addition to optometric vision therapy, Dr. Berne incorporates complementary practices such as cranial sacral therapy as well
as counseling on nutrition.

Drs. Marc Grossman and Glen Swartwout are co-authors of *Natural Eye Care: An Encyclopedia – Complementary Treatments for Improving and Saving Your Eyes* (Dr. Grossman is also a licensed acupuncturist; Dr. Swartwout's interests span the fields of biological medicine, nutrition and homeopathy). The two optometrists guide the reader through proper nutrition, acupuncture, acupressure and basic exercises for a variety of problems, including cataracts, glaucoma and macular degeneration.

Dr. Jacob Liberman, who has written several important books about vision, tells in *Take Off Your Glasses and See*, how he improved his own eyesight. He explores the relationship between energy and emotions and vision. Dr. R-M. Kaplan balances scientific concepts with an exploration of the mind/body influences of vision in *The Power Behind Your Eyes: Improving Your Eyesight With Integrated Vision Therapy* and guides readers through the process of understanding how vision is related to the bigger picture of one's life.

## Changing Old Habits

Optometric vision therapy for any patient, young or old, may begin by using procedures that start to break any bad visual habits, habits that have caused the eyes to work separately rather than together. Then, the optometrist teaches the individual how to use the eyes as a team. Step by step, the patient goes through all the learning stages necessary to achieve normal eye teaming. Most of us, with Nature's help, already have good teaming, but sometimes Nature needs a little help. Any optometric vision therapy can take a couple of months or many months—it all depends on the severity of the imbalance.

## Forty Countries Offer This Valuable Therapy

From Europe to Japan, Australia and New Zealand, the availability of optometric vision therapy has grown steadily. Sometimes optometrists from other countries come to study in the U.S. Often, practitioners from the U.S. travel widely to share their expertise. Dr. Greg Gilman of Quincy, California, traveled continuously for eighteen months around the world. He lectured in 25 countries and an average of seventy-five people attended each lecture, although once he had an audience of 2,500 optometrists. Dr. Glen Swartwout, now in Hilo, Hawaii, spent two years in Japan, as the first director of the Optometric Center of Tokyo, which he helped to found.

By the first decade of the 21st century, optometric vision therapy was offered in some forty countries, a number that grows exponentially. In the United States, most of the twenty colleges of optometry offer post-doctorate courses in vision therapy. Many also have clinics where optometric vision care is available. A number of institutions, such as the SUNY College of Optometry, the Eye Institute at the Pennsylvania College of Optometry and Southern California College of Optometry, place a strong emphasis on the value of teamwork. This was also the case at the internationally celebrated Gesell Institute of Human Development at Yale University in Connecticut. One of Gesell's four departments was devoted to vision.

## The Pioneers In Vision and Behavior

Many names stand out from the early days of behavioral optometry: Drs. Alexander, Brock, Getman, McCoy and Macdonald; their contributions have been integral to shaping this remarkable discipline. Yet there is one individual who is generally regarded as the "father" of behavioral optometry: A. M. Skeffington, O.D.

In the 1920s, Skeffington began to question what could be done for vision problems beyond the simple prescribing of lenses to wear. His creative mind reached out beyond the boundaries of his own field of optometry to involve authorities from other disciplines as diverse as biology, physiology, psychology, neurology, physics and education. From 1928, for forty years, Skeffington was the mainspring of the professional organization of optometrists, the Optometric Extension Program Foundation. The first organization to develop a wide variety of continuing education courses for its members and to publish education and information pamphlets for the public, the foundation is now international and sponsors conferences around the world.

Arnold Gesell, M.D., for whom Yale's Gesell Institute was named, was another of the early investigators who helped establish the foundations of this health care in the 1940s. Dr. Gesell, widely regarded as one of the world's leading pediatric psychologists and a specialist in child development, studied vision for almost a decade with a team of experts. The result was the landmark book, *Vision and Its Development In Infant and Child.*

Since then, the critical connection between vision and behavior has been painstakingly established and scientifically verified. Gradually the precepts of the optometric vision therapy as an invaluable health therapy have been developed:

- vision problems may trigger or aggravate learning or behavior problems as well as a range of health issues, including headaches, migraines, teeth-grinding and depression;
- vision can be trained;
- when vision is treated by optometric vision therapy, learning, behavior and health may also change and improve.

## The Pros and Cons of Home Vision Therapy

Often, when you are having optometric vision therapy, out-of-office or home vision procedures will be suggested as part of treatment—parents involved in such work with infants, preschool or schoolchildren often become dedicated to the therapy's concepts of prevention. However, regular office visits are important for a number of reasons. At an office, you have professionals who can analyze progress and adjust the activities where necessary. Also, the use of lenses, a critical factor in this therapy, needs to be monitored for adjustment.

The question of home procedures must always be considered carefully. Some children may need the help of an adult, but if the home situation isn't correct for that involvement, then it's wise to wait before starting work at home. Optometric vision therapy at home for adults is often recommended but the guidelines are the same as those for youngsters.

## Suzanna's Home Procedures

Suzanna was 5 years old when she was brought to Dr. E. Bertolli in Connecticut. She held reading materials extremely close to her eyes and also had difficulty following a slow moving object with her eyes. The test for depth perception, or stereopsis, showed that the child had very poor depth perception. Although one of her eyes was very farsighted, her visual acuity, or clearness of sight in that eye was exceedingly low 20/400 (legally blind is 20/200); the other eye measured 20/25.

After a year of vision therapy, much of it done at home from a CD that Dr. Bertolli made for the family because they lived at a distance from his office, supplemented by telephone calls, Suzanna had developed normal tracking skills and her depth perception (stereopsis) was in the normal range. She had also made excellent progress with her visual acuity, for now each eye measured 20/20. By this time, Suzanna was doing well in school and when she read, her posture was good, an important point because of the effect that posture has on our vision systems.

**Peripheral and Binocular Vision**. You may want to check these two vital areas. Peripheral vision, when used by both eyes simultaneously in a binocular manner, is one of the most important functions of your visual system. It lets you know where you are.

It is also the basis for the development of size, time and spatial concepts. If you know where you are when walking, balancing or running, you will not stagger or fall or bump into objects.

You can check your peripheral vision by standing in the middle of the room and looking straight ahead. Are you aware of all or some of the rest of the room? Ask a friend or someone in your family how much they notice of side areas when they look straight ahead.

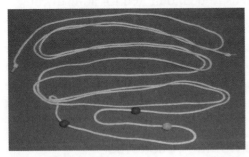

### The Brock String: A Simple Home Exercise

**The Brock String Test** This device, three to five beads or buttons of different colors on a piece of string some three to four feet long, was created by Dr. Frederick Brock, one of the pioneers in the field of optometric vision therapy. It is a good example of the type of simple equipment that can be used to exercise and stimulate the vision system. If possible, ask an optometrist about using the Brock String; the practitioner may have some suggestions for you. When you use the Brock string, you learn a number of things:

• are you using both eyes as a team all the time?

• which eye is the "stronger" or dominant eye?

• what is the quality of each eye's vision?

When you focus on different beads at different times, you can develop valuable eye-teaming skills.

## How to Use the Brock String

- Thread string through four or five beads, preferably large ones, and secure them so that they're evenly spaced one from the other.
- Position the first bead about twelve inches from the end of the string.
- Attach one end of the string at eye level to a doorknob or other convenient handle or hold it yourself. Wind the other end around your fingers.
- Hold the string taut, at arm's length, with the end wrapped around your finger and held against the middle of your nose.
- Look at the bead closest to you.

You can hold the Brock string still or rotate it for focusing and teaming work. If you are using both eyes together at the same time and aiming accurately at the first bead, it will look as if there are two strings that meet in a V at the bead. It will look as if the strings go into the beads and come out on the other side, thus forming an X. Each string should look to be of equal quality, not fuzzy or indistinct at any place.

If the strings meet before the bead, you have a tendency to *fixate* or aim *inaccurately* or *overconverge*. This will cause you to hold your reading material too close, which is stressful. It might also cause you to blur at distance occasionally. If the strings meet behind the button, you are *diverging*.

If you see two beads side by side, you have difficulty *converging*. This means you probably hold your reading too far away, causing stress. (Lower back problems may result.)

If your eyes do not work together as a team, you rarely know this. Where there's a lack of teaming, the individual often uses first one eye then the other—this is done at the cortical level, because it is your brain that is directing the action. If you are alternating the use of your eyes, using first one and then the other, the result is certain behavioral characteristics. You might change your mind a great deal or have difficulty making decisions. Perhaps you have a slow response to a visual exercise such as the Brock String. This often indicates a slow starter, maybe even someone accused of being a procrastinator. The stress of hidden visual problems such as poor teaming or alternating is often the trigger for disruptive behavior.

**Daily Use, If Possible** – If you find your binocularity is not very efficient, try to use the Brock string daily. Don't overdo it at first if you do have problems, such as the strings meeting in front of or behind the bead at which you aim your eyes. Just as you must gradually build up endurance for physical exercise, so you must build up endurance for visual exercise. At first, spend about 40 seconds on each bead, preferably at the same time each day and as many times a week as possible. Then, as you improve, you can slowly increase the time you take to do this simple but amazingly effective drill.

**Efficient Binocular Ability** – When you see two strings that are of the same quality, you have efficient binocular ability. Perhaps you have learned to see the strings in the correct place but they do not stay visible clearly or steadily but flicker or fade. If so, you need to work consistently at the drill to develop efficient eye teaming that allows you to use both eyes at the same time and have consistent vision.

It's shocking to realize one doesn't always see consistently. Normally, we are not aware of vision imbalances. It's only when we start using devices like the Brock string that we begin to realize the quality of our perceptions. If you are playing sports—football, tennis, golf, baseball—you may not time your swing at the ball correctly. Analyze your own game. If you see the strings on the Brock string cross behind the bead, you sometimes swing too late. If you see the strings cross in front of the bead, you tend to swing too early.

If our vision systems are not efficient, we need to put far more effort and energy into trying to have accurate perceptions than people who have good vision. When you are driving, your brain wants to know where the road is for the left-hand turn. If you cannot see the turn of the road accurately, you will analyze the information over and over in an attempt to understand the visual input. This can be dangerous when you're behind the wheel of a car. In many situations, it can make you seem slow, even stupid.

**Test Your Binocular Vision** — A simple way to check if you do use both eyes at the same time can be done at home with the cardboard tube from, say, a roll of paper towel.

1. Hold the cardboard tube in one hand, position it in front of one eye and look through the tube.
2. Place your free hand, palm facing you, halfway down, at the center of the tube, by the side of the tube.
3. If you are using both eyes together, you will see a hole in your palm, which matches the size of the hole that you see at the end of the tube.
4. If you are not using both eyes together, you will either look down the cardboard tube or just see your hand.

**Conclusion.** You have efficient binocular vision if you see both the tube and the hole in your palm at the same time. You are not truly binocular if you see only one or the other, if the tube and the circle are not equally distinct, or if the images blur or fade in and out. You probably knew this if you are unable to view 3-D movies.

What does this lack of true binocularity mean? It means that you do not have accurate depth perception. This imbalance is a drain on energy. It also leads to stress. It creates difficulties in your perception of your location and the location of objects around you. Walking, driving or sports activities become obstacle courses.

## A Multitude of Home Procedures

The range of home procedures is considerable. Some make use of simple objects, balls on strings, pencils, dowels; others are sophisticated. Usually, lenses are an integral part of any program. Sometimes nasal occluders (nasal or binasal tapes) are used on lenses to treat myopia, strabismus, amblyopia and suppression. Nasal or binasal occluders are tapes of varying widths; they are applied to spectacles to disrupt the wearer's visual habits and bring desirable changes. Practice is needed if there are to be improvements in the way individuals use their vision systems.

# 10

# Your Infant's Vision

Most babies are born with healthy eyes, free from disease and vision problems. Learning to *use* those eyes is one of the critical first steps in a newborn's development.

Since infants spend a large part of their time learning to see, parents of new babies will be glad to read there's a lot they can do to help infants develop healthy vision systems.

Whether it's the presence of bright wallpaper, the frequent repositioning of the crib, or a colorful mobile to provide variety and movement, the points are simple and effective. The sources of the following suggestions are the American Optometric Association's background paper on infants' vision and the guidelines developed over many years at the Infants' Vision Clinic at the College of Optometry, State University of New York, in New York City, under the direction of Elliott Forrest, O.D.

## A Home Guide for Parents

## Early Visual Stimulation

- Keep a dim light burning in the nursery at night so that the infant will have something to look at upon awakening.

- Move the crib regularly, as well as the baby's position in the crib so that light will stimulate each eye. It's preferable to use clear bumper guards so vision is not obstructed.

- Approach, change, feed and even play with the baby from different positions. Talk to your baby as you move around the room; this gives the infant a moving object to follow. During the day, place the child in different rooms so that new sights, objects, patterns and different lights will stimulate the vision system.

- For the first two months, keep a bright mobile dangling outside the crib to provide variety and movement. At about eight weeks, move the mobile over the crib so the baby can touch it. This permits reinforcement of tactual and visual information.

## Hand-Eye Coordination

- Play peek-a-boo and play patty-cake.
- Provide blocks, rattles, balls and other toys for the baby to touch, bang and throw. Use objects large enough so they can't be swallowed. As the child gets older, make available toys (including pots and pans) to stack, nest, build, string, toss, push, pull, pound, take apart and put together. Clay or Play-Doh™, puzzles, tracing and coloring are also good.

## General Visual-Motor Coordination

- Give the child freedom to explore. Avoid the restraints of a playpen, crib or high chair when they are not required. Let the child move around as much as possible.
- Encourage the child to wiggle, roll, crawl and creep. This helps coordinate the two sides of the body efficiently, an ability that is reflected in the coordination of the two eyes.
- Parents, therefore, ought not to encourage their babies to walk before the crawling and creeping phases.
- Set up an obstacle course of boxes, chairs and tables so that the child can creep under, over and between objects.
- When the child can walk, encourage the use of a wheelbarrow or some other push-and-balance toy.
- Encourage the child to run, jump, balance, hop and climb.

## Match Vision With Other Sensory Motor Systems

- Whenever possible, talk and play with the child. Tell stories and sing songs together.
- Offer different objects and have the child tell which is heavier, lighter or noisier when dropped.

These are some of the ways you can help get your child's vision system off to a healthy start. It cannot be repeated often enough: the child has to learn to see. We are not born with sophisticated visual abilities. Adults can depend on vision alone to discriminate and understand the size, shape, texture and weight of objects. Infants need help to understand this type of information. They are dependent in the learning process on touching, feeling, squeezing—tactile evidence that allows them to confirm what their vision notes.

As children grow, they will start to base their judgments of texture, shape, size and weight of objects on visual assessment alone. The sight of a ball will trigger their memories of how it feels and what it weighs without the need for tactile evidence that was necessary earlier. In those early stages, the infant's vision system must be carefully nurtured for balanced development.

## Infant Vision Needs Examination, Too

Perhaps the most important safeguard recommended by the AOA is that unless signs of problems occur earlier, a child's first thorough vision examination needs to be given by the time your child is three years old. The wisest choice is to go to the best qualified eye doctor, the optometrist who specializes in behavioral, developmental or functional optometry.

This examination will cover more than simply determining that the child's eyes are healthy, with the ability to rate well, even as high as 20/20 on the eye chart. It will examine the total vision system to make sure that it is in balance and functioning efficiently and at the appropriate level for a three-year-old. The examination is best repeated again before the youngster enters school and annually thereafter until adulthood.

## The InfantSEE® Program

A no-cost public health program, InfantSEE® was created in an effort to encourage optometric infant eye and vision assessments and ensure that professional eye care is available for infants across the U.S. and accessible to everyone. It is supported by Optometry's Charity™ - The AOA Foundation, the American Optometric Association (AOA), and The Vision Care Institute™, a Johnson & Johnson company. Optometrists provide a one-time, comprehensive eye assessment to infants in their first year of life through InfantSEE®. Usually, this means that infants are examined between the ages of

6 and 12 months. This offers early detection of potential eye and vision problems at no cost, regardless of income or ability to pay.

**The program's objectives:**

- identify and treat risk factors that may have adverse effects on eye and vision health;
- reduce the impact of eye and visual conditions that may lead to impairments and/or loss of sight, and may also affect the child's social, emotional, and cognitive development;
- educate parents about the importance of eye care for their children.

Vision plays a significant role in overall development, early identification and rapid response and the specialized care offered through InfantSEE® will minimize the long-term impact of any visual conditions that may develop. Parents may find more information and locate a provider in their area by visiting www.infantsee.org and clicking on the icon "Find an InfantSEE® Doctor" at the top of the page, entering a zip code and adjusting the search radius (1 to 100 miles). Or you can call toll-free, 888-396-EYES (3937), to obtain a list of providers in your vicinity.

The Mission Statement of InfantSEE® explains that it is a public health program designed to ensure that optometric eye and vision care becomes an integral part of infant wellness care to improve a child's quality of life.

## A Premature Infant's Cerebral Palsy

Rupert was 10 years old when his occupational therapist referred him to Dr. Michele Hlava, of Somerset West, South Africa, because the youngster was struggling with reading, reversing letters and words. A premature baby, born at 30 weeks by epidural caesarean section, Rupert was eventually diagnosed with cerebral palsy.This may have been the result of an apnea attack (when he stopped breathing) due to septicemia. As a result, his left arm and hand had very tight or spastic muscles; Rupert also had signs of partial paralysis of one side of the body (spastic hemiplegia).

Rupert's first smile only came at 4 months. At 5 months his mother knew there was a problem: his legs were crossed over each other and his back appeared to be spastic. By the time he was 7 months old, Rupert still could not sit; by the time he was 2, he was only able to pull himself along on his arms. He started to learn to walk by the time he was 10.

Dr. Hlava's vision exam revealed that Rupert had a convergence insufficiency (when you aim the eyes at an object at close distance, both eyes should be able to track accurately an object moving towards them until the object is within an inch of the nose). This vision imbalance caused him to lose concentration and become frustrated with schoolwork (as if Rupert needed this, on top of his developmental difficulties and cerebral palsy).

An intensive optometric visual therapy program was begun with a program that was home-based because the family lived hundreds of miles from Dr. Hlava. After 3 months of vision therapy, Rupert had a 6-month break from the vision therapy and at the end of that period was reassessed by Dr. Hlava. She found that the youngster had maintained the progress he had made in balancing his vision. The happy result was that his schoolwork and behavior in class had improved. Rupert did, however, continue with occupational therapy.

# Appendix – How to Find Help

**The American Academy of Optometry**
110 Executive Blvd., Ste. 506
Rockville, MD 20852
www.aaopt.org
The Academy was founded in 1922 with the express purpose of fostering the continued advancement of the education and knowledge of optometrists.

**The American Optometric Association (AOA)**
243 N. Lindbergh Blvd..
St. Louis, MO 63141
www.aoa.org
Founded in 1898, the AOA is a federation of local associations representing more than 24,000 doctors of optometry in the U.S.

**The Australasian College of Behavioural Optometry (ACBO)**
112 Yarrara Rd.
Pennant Hills, New South Wales, 2120
Australia
www.acbo.org.au
Optometrists in Australia, New Zealand and Asia founded ACBO in 1987 to provide education in the field of behavioural optometry.

**The College of Optometrists in Vision Development (COVD)**
215 W. Garfield Rd., Ste. 200
Aurora, OH 44202
www.covd.org
A non-profit, international association of eye care professionals, including optometrists, optometry students and vision therapists, COVD was established in 1971.

### The College of Syntonic Photo-Optometry

The charter of this nonprofit organization is to promote the therapeutic use of light to the clinical practice of optometrists through postgraduate education and research. Established in 1933 by H. R. Spitler, M.D., O.D., it is now international and provides basic and advanced education at its annual conferences on light and vision. www.syntonicphototherapy.com

### The Optometric Extension Program Foundation (OEPF)
1921 E. Carnegie, Ste. 3-L
Santa Ana, CA 92705-5811
www.oepf.org

International in scope, OEPF was founded in 1928 and is the principal provider of postgraduate education to optometrists. It publishes pamphlets for the general consumer as well as the *Journal of Behavioral Optometry*. Listed below are their five most popular pamphlets (use the number after the description to order from OEPF).

- **When a Bright Child Has Trouble Reading.** A mother's story of her efforts to deal with an undiagnosed, learning-related visual problem and the effectiveness of lenses and visual training in solving the problem. **A128**

- **What Is Vision Therapy?** Explains the visual skills and how each affects people's performance in all aspects of life. Provides overview of what behavioral optometrists do to improve visual performance. **B114**

- **Does Your Child Have a Learning-related Vision Problem?** Simple-to-use checklist of signals to help parents and teachers recognize if a child has learning-related visual difficulties. **B116**

- **Attention Deficit Disorder: A Developmental Approach** by Patricia Lemer, M.Ed.
  Discusses the definition, symptoms and different treatment regimens for Attention Deficit Hyperactivity Disorder (ADHD). Includes descriptions of vision therapy, occupational therapy and treatment of allergies, and a simple chart illustrating symptoms associated with diagnoses of ADHD, Sensory Integration Dysfunction, Learning-related Visual Problems, Nutrition and Allergies. References. **B121**

- **Educator's Guide & Checklist to Classroom Vision Problems.** An explanation of the visual functions involved in classroom tasks and checklist of observations and symptoms indicative of visual problems related to learning disabilities. **B201**

**Parents Active for Vision Education (PAVE)**
4135 54th Place
San Diego, CA 92105
www.pave.org
www.pavevision.org

PAVE was created in 1988 by Marjie Thompson, the parent of a child whose life was changed by vision therapy. Marjie worked as a therapist in the California practice of optometrists Drs. Sanet, Hillier and Treganza. PAVE's purpose is to "raise awareness among children, parents, educators and the medical community of the critical relationship between vision and achievement." Marjie urged that all children be tested for the four Fs (focusing, fusion, fixation and form perception) before being taught the three Rs.

**The Neuro-Optometric Rehabilitation Association (NORA)**
1921 E. Carnegie, Ste. 3L
Santa Ana, CA 92705
www.nora.cc/

An international, multidisciplinary organization, NORA was established in 1989 to provide and advocate for vision rehabilitation and the habilitation of neurologically challenged individuals through the understanding and applications of the current principles in vision science.

## Recommended Reading

Barry, Susan R. *Fixing My Gaze – A Scientist's Journey into Seeing in Three Dimensions.* Basic Books, 2009.

Berne, Samuel, A. *Without Ritalin, A Natural Approach to ADD.* Keats Publishing. 2006. Orders: Colorstone Press, 227 E. Palace Ave., Ste. G, Santa Fe, New Mexico, 87501. www.holisticvision. org.

Gallop, S., *Looking Differently at Nearsightedness and Myopia: The Visual Process and the Myth of 20/20.* Available at www.oepf. org & www.GallopIntoVision.com.

Kaplan, Melvin. *Seeing Through New Eyes: Changing the Lives of Children with Autism, Asperger Syndrome and Other Developmental Disabilities Through Vision Therapy.* Jessica Kingsley Publishers, 2006.

Kurtz, Lisa A. *Visual Perception Problems in Children with AD/HD, Autism, and Other Learning Disabilities: A Guide for Parents and Professionals.* Jessica Kingsley Publishers, 2006.

Note: In his review of the book by Lisa A. Kurtz (*Journal of Behavioral Optometry*, 2007; 18:4:107), Dr. Marc B. Taub wrote, "Parents, teachers, schools systems, and the medical community are increasingly looking for resources to help guide them in treatment and management [of those with learning disabilities, including autism and AD/HD]. The author of this book has been a pediatric occupational therapist for over three decades and is a former Director of Occupational Therapy for the Children's Hospital of Philadelphia.

"In her introduction, Ms. Kurtz states that the purpose of the book is to guide parents, teachers and others who work with children with developmental delays to better understand how to: 1) recognize and screen for subtle problems, 2) understand the options that are available, 3) learn strategies for coping with problems at home and school, 4) identify additional resources for learning more about these issues."

Lemer, Patricia, S., Editor, *Envisioning a Bright Future, Interventions that Work for Children and Adults with Autism Spectrum Disorders.* This is the most comprehensive book on autism treatment presently available. It offers an unparalleled gathering of individual chapters by twenty informed authors whose expertise covers the spectrum of professionals caring for those with autism. Available at: www.oepf.org.

## DVDs

Berne, Samuel, A. "ADD to Autism: Reaching Your Child's Potential—Naturally." Colorstone Press, 227 E. Palace Ave., Ste. G, Santa Fe, New Mexico, 87501.

# Scientific Studies

*Bibliography of Near Lenses and Vision Training Research,* published by the OEP Foundation; over 1,500 references in 64 categories related to the functional, developmental and behavioral aspects of optometric vision care. The research in the *Bibliography* has been published in over 200 publications, including the *New England Journal of Medicine,* the *British Journal of Ophthalmology,* the *Canadian Journal of Surgery,* the *Australian Orthoptic Journal,* the *Scandinavian Journal of Psychology* and the *South Africa Medical Journal.* OEPBIB 90-3

Bowan, M.D. Learning disabilities, dyslexia, and vision: a subject review. A rebuttal, literature review, and commentary. *Optometry,* 2002; 73:553-75.

Ciuffreda, K.J. The scientific basis for and efficacy of optometric vision therapy in nonstrabismic accommodative and vergence disorders. *Optometry,* 2002; 73: 735-762.

Maples, W.C. Visual factors that significantly impact academic performance. *Optometry,* 2003; 4:35-49.

Press, L.J. Guest Editorial, *Journal of Behavioral Optometry,* 2005; 16(2): 48.

Rutner, D.M., Kapoor, N., Ciuffreda, K.J., Suchoff, I.B., et al, Frequency of Occurrence and Treatment of Ocular Disease in Symptomatic Individuals with Acquired Brain Injury, A Clinical Management Perspective. *Journal of Behavioral Optometry,* 2007; 18(2): 31-36.

Scheiman, M., Mitchell, G.L., Cotter, S., et al: The Convergence Insufficiency Treatment Trial (CITT)Study Group. A randomized clinical trial of treatments for convergence insufficiency in children. *Archives of Ophthalmology* 2005; 123: 14-24.

Scheiman, M., Cotter, S., et al. Randomized Clinical Trial of Treatments for Symptomatic Convergence Insufficiency in Children. *Archives of Ophthalmology,* 2008; 126(10):1139-336.

Zaba, J.N., Johnson, R.A., and Reynolds, W.T. Vision examinations for all children entering public school - the new Kentucky law. *Optometry*, 2003; 74:149-58.

For a wide selection of information from various sources such as Dr. L. J. Press, Dr. J. Metzger and others: www.visiontherapy.org/vision-therapy/faq

To find a range of informative material, including the full article, "The Myth of Critical Periods," Google Paul Harris, O.D.

## Colleges of Optometry (by State)

Information about the Association of Schools and Colleges of Optometry is at www.opted.org. You can find Canadian and foreign schools by going to the Affiliate Member page on that site.

**Illinois College of Optometry**
3241 South Michigan Avenue
Chicago, Illinois 60616
http://www.ico.edu

**Indiana University, School of Optometry**
800 East Atwater Avenue
Bloomington, Indiana 47401
http://www.opt.indiana.edu

**Inter American University of Puerto Rico, School of Optometry**
500 John Will Harris Rd.
Bayamon, Puerto Rico 00957
http://www.optonet.inter.edu

**Michigan College of Optometry at Ferris State University**
1310 Cramer Circle
Big Rapids, Michigan 49307-2738
http://www.ferris.edu/mco

**Midwestern University – Arizona College of Optometry**
19555 N. 59th Avenue
Glendale, Arizona 85308
http://www.midwestern.edu/AZCOPT/

## New England College of Optometry
424 Beacon Street
Boston, Massachusetts 02115
http://www.neco.edu

## Northeastern State University – Oklahoma College of Optometry
College of Optometry
1001 North Grand Avenue
Tahlequah, Oklahoma 74464
http://arapaho.nsuok.edu/~optometry

## Nova Southeastern University
Health Professions Division
College of Optometry
3200 S. University Drive
Ft. Lauderdale, Florida 33328
http://www.nova.edu

## The Ohio State University College of Optometry
338 West Tenth Avenue
Columbus, Ohio 43210
http://optometry.osu.edu

## Pacific University
## College of Optometry
2043 College Way
Forest Grove, Oregon 97116
http://www.opt.pacificu.edu

## Pennsylvania College of Optometry at Salus University
Elkins Park Campus
8360 Old York Road
Elkins Park, Pennsylvania 19027-1598
http://www.salus.edu

## Southern California College of Optometry
2575 Yorba Linda Boulevard
Fullerton, California 92831
http://www.scco.edu

**Southern College of Optometry**
1245 Madison Avenue
Memphis, Tennessee 38104
http://www.sco.edu

**State University of New York, State College of Optometry**
33 West 42nd Street
New York, New York 10036-8003
http://www.sunyopt.edu

**University of Alabama at Birmingham School of Optometry**
1716 University Boulevard
Birmingham, Alabama 35294-0010
http://www.uab.edu/optometry

**University of California – Berkeley, School of Optometry**
Admissions & Student Affairs Office
397 Minor Hall
Berkeley, California 94720-2020
http://optometry.berkeley.edu

**University of Missouri at St. Louis, College of Optometry**
One University Boulevard
St. Louis, Missouri 63121-4499
http://www.umsl.edu/divisions/optometry

**University of Houston**
**College of Optometry**
505 J. Davis Armistead Building
Houston, Texas 77204-2020
http://www.opt.uh.edu

**University of the Incarnate Word, School of Optometry**
4301 Broadway
San Antonio, Texas 78209-6397
http://optometry.uiw.edu

**Western University of Health Sciences,**
**College of Optometry**
309 E. Second Street
Pomona, California 91766-1854
http://www.westernu.edu

# Index

# About the Authors

**Hazel Richmond Dawkins** is a veteran editor-writer whose career began in London's Fleet Street newspaper world and has since taken her to Paris, Geneva and New York City. She has worked for major publishers, including Harper &Row (now HarperCollins) and Columbia University Press.

**Ellis S. Edelman, O.D.**, received his Doctorate in Optometry from the Pennsylvania College of Optometry and is a graduate of the Gesell Institute's postdoctoral course in behavioral optometry. An associate of the College of Vision Development and the OEP Foundation, Dr. Edelman specializes in optometric vision care at Newtown Square, Pennsylvania.

**Constantine Forkiotis, O.D.**, was a classmate of Dr Edelman at both the Pennsylvania College of Optometry and Yale's Gesell Institute. A Fellow of the American Academy of Optometry and the College of Vision Development, until his death in 2007, he was active in many organizations, including the Connecticut State Board of Education.

The Connecticut State Police have used the behavioral optometric vision programs Dr. Forkiotis developed for them since 1970.

A consultant for the U.S. Department of Transportation Research Office and the National Health Traffic Safety Administration for drug-testing detection and the National Standardized Behavioral Sobriety tests, Dr. Forkiotis was invited by the State of Iowa to present an expert witness course to police training officers, state prosecuting attorneys, country attorneys and behavioral optometrists in 1985. Continuing his work, Drs. Bertolli and Pannone lecture at the Connecticut State Police Academy, offering the courses in the pioneering work of their mentor, Dr. Forkiotis.

# Reviews of
# The Suddenly Successful Student

"A great book that stands the test of time, especially with the addition of new updated material. This is a far-reaching, easy to read source of information that students of all ages and those who care for them should not be without. If you are already struggling at school or at work or want to prevent problems before they start, read this book."
  Steve Gallop, O.D., FCOVD
  Author: *Looking Differently at Nearsightedness and Myopia: The Visual Process and the Myth of 20/20*

"Despite years of continuous success in aiding children and adults with visually related learning and performance problems, many parents and teachers are still unaware of the magnitude of optometric contributions to this important area. This book attempts to fill that gap."
  Elliott B. Forrest, O.D., Infants' Vision Clinic,
  College of Optometry, State University of New York

"At last, a handbook for the general reader, and it's good enough to recommend for my courses."
  Charles B. Margach, O.D., Professor of Optometry,
  Southern California College of Optometry

"...aimed at the general public...succeeds admirably, discussing the history and background of optometric vision training...."
  Martin H. Birnbaum, O.D., New York

"A readable and thorough presentation of visual dysfunction which often results in significant learning difficulties and behavioral problems in children, adolescents and adults."
  Morris Wessel, M.D., Pediatrician
  Clinical Professor Emeritus of Pediatrics, Yale-New Haven,
  Connecticut

"I learned a lot. Even general practitioners need to know the applications of optometric vision therapy to avoid prolonging patients' problems."
  Dorothea Linley, M.D., General Practitioner,
  Connecticut

*The Suddenly Successful Student & Friends* is an important, easy read. The small book contains down-to-earth information that has the potential to positively affect the lives of both children and adults.

The message the book elegantly presents is the importance and value of vision therapy to positively affect abilities, achievement and quality of life. The book's central concept is to describe vision therapy as well as to review the related scientific background and research. It highlights the importance and complexity of an updated view of vision function and its influence on one's ability and success. A key goal of the book is to explain the difference between sight and the complexities of vision.

Vision therapy is a program of treatment and dynamic education to promote enhancement of human vision development. Its purpose is to guide and teach more effective decision-making and behavior.

Vision therapy has an extensive history of producing many remarkable instances of changes in an individual's life. I have spent over 60 years clinically involved in vision therapy in private practice, as a staff member and director of vision research at the Gesell Institute of Child Development on the campus of Yale, working in public schools, teaching at universities and participating in a nonprofit research center. My experience has verified the complex process of human vision and the power vision enhancement has in changing people's lives.

I describe vision as the prevailing behavior of the sighted human. It is an activator to define orientation, localization, controlling eye movements and focusing. It is a receptor in that it reaches out to interact and receive external information. Vision directs looking, seeing, movement, attention and thinking. It is an overseer of human actions and both directs and derives meaning in one's perceived environment.

One of my favorite summaries is: "When vision is working well, it leads and guides all that we do; when not, it interferes." The book, *The Suddenly Successful Student & Friends,* is a gold mine of information and valuable guidance to help parents, teachers and other professionals.

John W. Streff, O.D., D.O.S.
Author: *Childhood Learning: Journey or Race?*
Former Director, Vision Research at Yale's Gesell Institute.